THE COMPLETE BACHELOR

Manners for Men

Walter Germain Robinson

summersdale

THE COMPLETE BACHELOR: MANNERS FOR MEN

First published by D. Appleton and Company in 1896
This revised edition published in 2016 by Summersdale Publishers Ltd
Images © Shutterstock or out of copyright

Summersdale Publishers Ltd
46 West Street
Chichester
West Sussex
PO19 1RP
UK

www.summersdale.com

Printed and bound in the Czech Republic

ISBN: 978-1-84953-816-9

Substantial discounts on bulk quantities of Summersdale books are available to corporations, professional associations and other organisations. For details contact Nicky Douglas by telephone: +44 (0) 1243 756902, fax: +44 (0) 1243 786300 or email: nicky@summersdale.com.

PREFACE

I suppose a book of this character needs some excuse. The world is full of volumes written on etiquette, and, in adding another to the number, my plea for filling the want long felt may seem ridiculous. But I have an excellent reason, and that is, that in all treatises of this character I have found the bachelor sadly neglected.

I have endeavored to be plain and lucid. I only desired that this book should be a help to my reader in any dilemma of social import, and if I shall have proved of assistance, I shall feel that my mission has been accomplished, and that I have reached the goal of my ambition.

Walter Germain Robinson

CONTENTS

Chapter I

THE BACHELOR
IN PUBLIC

ASSISTING A LADY IN PUBLIC

The average man is judged by his appearance and his deportment in public. His dress, his bearing, his conduct toward women and his fellow-men, are telling characteristics.

In the street, when walking with a woman—the term "lady" being objectionable, except in case of distinction—every man should be on his mettle. Common sense, which is the basis of all etiquette, teaches him that he should be her protector. Therefore, under general circumstances, his place is on the street or outer side. Should there be a crowd on the inner side, should the walking be muddy or rough, or should there be a building in process of repair, or one or the other of the inconveniences of city life, then the man should take the side which will enable him to shield his fair companion from all annoyance. At night a man offers his arm to a woman. In the daytime etiquette allows this only when the sidewalk is very rough, when there are steps to climb, a crowd to be piloted through, or a street crossing to effect. In any one of these emergencies suggest, "I think you will find it better to take my arm." A man never walks bodkin—that is, sandwiched between two women.

When escorting a woman to a house where she is to make a visit, always mount the stoop or steps with her, ring the bell, and remain there until the servant comes to the door. Then, if you are not going in, take off your hat and leave her.

MANNERLY INTRODUCTIONS

It is the privilege of a woman to bow first. She may have reasons why she should not wish to continue an acquaintance, and a man should never take the initiative. Abroad, in many countries, the man bows first. When old friends meet, however, the bowing is simultaneous.

A man lifts his hat in acknowledgment of any salutation made to the woman with whom he is walking. It is his place, on such an occasion, to bow to a man friend, whether the latter enjoys or does not have the pleasure of the acquaintance of the woman. A man's failure to do this signifies that the woman does not wish to know him, or that her companion does not wish her to know the other man.

It is not good form to stop a woman on the street, even if the exchange of a few commonplace remarks be the excuse. A man never joins a woman on a thoroughfare unless she be one from whose friendship he is sure that he can claim this privilege.

A gentleman always assists a woman in and out of a carriage or a public conveyance. He opens the door of the vehicle for her, helps her in by a deft motion of the right arm, and with his left protects her skirts from any possible mud or dust on the wheel. As he leaves her he closes the door, and, if it be a private conveyance, gives directions to the driver. He lifts his hat in bidding her good-by. Even when there is a footman, a second man, or an attendant, it should be esteemed a favor to give this assistance.

A man always rises from the table at which he is sitting when a woman bows to him and immediately returns the salutation. Should the place be in the open, he doffs his hat, which under such circumstances he is obliged to wear. When he is in a party and a lady and her escort chance to stop at his table to exchange greetings with his friends, he should rise and remain standing during the conversation. If a man is introduced to him, unattended by a woman, and he is with a stag party, politeness bids him also rise.

WHEN TO USE THE 'LADIES FIRST' RULE

In entering shops, theaters, or other buildings, where there are swinging doors, the escort goes ahead and holds one of them ajar, passing in last. A woman always precedes a man, except in one or two special cases. A man precedes a woman walking down the aisle of a theater, and it is better form that he should take the inside seat, especially if there is a man occupying the place next to the vacant one. A man precedes a woman up a narrow staircase in a public building, but in a private house, in ascending or descending a stairway, he should always allow the woman to precede him. In entering a theater box a man follows the usher, preceding the woman down the theater corridor to the door of the box. He then holds this open, and the women precede him, he following them. In a church, in going down a narrow aisle, the woman precedes the man.

CONVENTIONS OF HAT-TIPPING

Hotel corridors and halls may be classed as semi-public places. A man meeting a woman in one of these, where by custom he is permitted to keep on his hat, must step aside and let her pass, raising his hat as he does so. This does not apply to theater corridors, theater or hotel lobbies, or offices. In such houses as the Waldorf in New York, where the hall is utilized as a general sitting room by both sexes, it is not good form for a man to keep on his hat. In London, however, the rule is not as strict.

Men in this country do not lift their hats to one another, except when they are introduced in the open or a public place. Civility is never wasted, and it is proper, as well as an act of reverence, to thus salute a clergyman or a venerable and distinguished gentleman.

A man always lifts his hat when offering a woman a service, such as picking up or restoring to her a dropped pocket handkerchief or other article, or when passing a fare in a public conveyance, or when rendering any trifling assistance. Should she be with a male escort, the latter should raise his hat and thank the person who has rendered the service. This bit of politeness is under no circumstances the prelude to an acquaintance with an unescorted woman, and no gentleman would take advantage of it. A man always raises his hat and remains uncovered when talking to a woman.

The lift or elevator, as well as the corridors and lobbies of a public building, the office of a hotel, and the vestibule of a theater, are public highways. In these places a man keeps on his hat, his deportment being the same as he would observe in the street. But when the lift or elevator is fitted up as a drawing room, such as is used in hotels and other semi-public buildings, a man removes his hat when the other sex is of the number of its passengers.

A TIP FROM THE AUTHOR

A gentleman will never be seen in public with characters whom he could not introduce to his mother or his sister. A man when he is with a lady should be very careful, especially at roof gardens and such places in midsummer, about recognizing male acquaintances who seem to be in rather doubtful company.

ESSENTIAL ACCESSORIES

In walking, a man should carry either a stick or a well-rolled umbrella. The stick should be grasped just below the crook or knob, but the ferrule must be kept downward. In business hours or on business thoroughfares to carry a stick is an affectation, but the man of leisure is regarded leniently in these abodes as a privileged character.

The umbrella is an instrument of peace rather than a weapon of war, and should not be carried as "trailed arms," but like the stick it should be grasped a short distance below the handle, and the latter held almost upright on a very slight perpendicular.

NO SMOKING

In the presence of ladies, unless by special permission, a gentleman never smokes, and under no circumstances does he indulge in a weed while on the street or walking with them. If, while smoking, a man should meet a woman and there should be any stopping to talk, he must at once throw away his cigar or his cigarette. A pipe is never smoked on fashionable promenades, and a man in a top hat and a frock coat with a pipe in his mouth is an anomaly. The pipe accompanies tweeds and a "pot" hat in the country or on business thoroughfares. A meerschaum or a wooden pipe is then allowable, but never a clay or a dudeen. The cuspidor is a banished instrument. The filthy custom of tobacco chewing and consequent expectoration can not be tolerated in civilized society.

GAIT AND POISE

A gentleman is never hurried, nor does he loiter. The fashionable gait is comparatively slow, with long steps. The exaggerated stride of the Anglomaniac is as bad form as the swagger of the Bowery "tough." The correct demeanor is without gesture or apparent effort.

Staring at or ogling women, standing at the entrances of theaters, churches, or other public buildings, stopping still and turning back to look at some one or something in the street, can be classified as offenses of which no gentleman can be guilty.

Free and easy attitudes are not tolerated in good society, and this same rule should apply to public conveyances. As the man who crosses his legs in the presence of ladies is absolutely impossible, so should be the individual who commits the same crime in a public conveyance. He not only proves a nuisance to those around him, but he is a source of damage as well as danger to the comfort and safety of his fellow-passengers.

APPROPRIATE BEHAVIOR IN PUBLIC CONVEYANCES

In a crowded car, ferryboat, or stage, it is yet a mooted question as to whether or not a man should give up his seat to a woman. In theory he should, but there are circumstances under which he may be pardoned. To a refined or delicate lady, to an old or an enfeebled woman, or one burdened with bundles or with a baby in the arms, the answer to this should be a decided affirmative. In public conveyances a man should sit to the right of a woman.

An escort should pay all fares in public conveyances, and should look after the comfort and welfare of his companion, taking entire charge of tickets, luggage, and luggage checks. Should a woman insist upon paying her *pro rata* of the expenses the arrangement can be made before starting, many sensible women handing their escorts their purses for the purpose. Do not offer to pay the fare of any of your women friends who might possibly enter your train or stage. This is embarrassing and not necessary. A railway car or carriage being a public conveyance, a man always keeps on his hat, as he also does in a cab or any other vehicle in which he is driving, accompanied or not accompanied by one of the opposite sex.

Chapter II

HOW A
BACHELOR
SHOULD DRESS

THE BASICS

There are three rules of dress which, for the ordinary man in his everyday life, might be resolved into two. These originally are morning, afternoon, and evening. Morning and evening are absolutely necessary; afternoon dress is donned on special occasions only.

DRESSING FOR EVERYDAY EVENTS

Morning dress is that which is worn during business hours or at any time in any place, where semiformal dress is not required until candlelight or seven o'clock in the evening. It consists usually in winter of a lounge or single-breasted sack suit made of many different kinds of material, the favorites being Scotch tweeds or black and blue cheviots, rough-faced and smooth. Fashions are liable to some variation season after season, and the general rule can only be laid down in a book of this kind.

With the morning or lounge dress in winter is worn the Derby or soft-felt Alpine hat, called the Hombourg. The Derbies are black, brown, or drab, and the felts are gray, brown, drab, or black. The colored shirt with white standing or turned-down collar is the usual accompaniment to the lounge suit. The fashion for colored shirts in stripes has been that the patterns run up and down and not across the bosom. The tie is a four-in-hand or an Ascot, or a simple bow, the boots black leather or dark-brown russet, and the gloves of tan or gray undressed kid or of dogskin. For ordinary business wear, suits of black or gray mixed cheviot, vicuña or worsted, or fancy Scotch goods, the coat of which is a "cutaway," are also popular; but the black diagonal "cutaway" has passed entirely out of fashion, and is utilized at present in riding costume.

IN SUMMER

The lounge suit in summer is of blue flannel or very light cheviot or tweed. Straw hats are worn in place of Derbies and felts. Fashion sometimes dictates fancy waistcoats of linen to be worn with business suits; otherwise the entire costume—trousers, coat, and waistcoat—is of the same material.

In the country, at the seaside, or in communities where golf, wheeling, tennis, yachting or other sports and pastimes are the order of the day, the costumes appropriate for these are in vogue for lounge or morning suits. This is what the English call "mufti." Such costumes are, however, not in good form in the city.

Black leather, tan, or russet shoes are worn with morning dress. White duck or flannel trousers, with black or blue cheviot coat and waistcoat, make fashionable lounge suits for summer resorts.

DRESSING FOR FORMAL OCCASIONS

Afternoon dress consists of a double-breasted frock coat of soft cheviot, vicuña, or diagonal worsted with either waistcoat to match—single-breasted or double-breasted—of fancy cloth, Marseilles duck or piqué; trousers of different material, usually cashmere, quiet in tone, with a striped pattern on a dark gray, drab, or blue background; boots of patent leather, buttoned, not tied; a white or colored shirt with straight standing white collar; a four-in-hand, puffed Ascot, or small club tie; silk hat and undressed gray, tan, or brown kid gloves. The colored shirt is an innovation, and it should be used sparingly, white linen on any semiformal function being in better form. When spats are used they should be of brown, gray, or drab cloth or canvas, to match the trousers as nearly as possible. Some ultra faddists wear white kid gloves with afternoon dress, but the fashion is not universal.

Afternoon dress is the attire for weddings—for the bridegroom, best man, ushers, and male guests; at afternoon teas, afternoon receptions, afternoon calls, afternoon walks on the fashionable avenue, garden parties (but not picnics), luncheons, and, in fact, at all formal or semiformal functions taking place between midday and candlelight, as well as at church on Sundays, at funerals, and in the park in London after midday.

Gray frock-coat suits are recent introductions from London, and have been worn at all the functions at which the black is required, but the latter is more conservative and in better taste. The afternoon dress is seldom worn in midsummer, morning suits being allowable at seaside and mountain-resort day functions.

DRESSING FOR FORMAL SOIREES

Evening dress is the proper attire, winter or summer, on all occasions after candlelight. There are two kinds of evening dress, formal and informal.

Formal or "full" evening dress, as it is sometimes vulgarly called, consists of the evening or "swallowtail" coat of black dress worsted or soft-faced vicuña, with or without silk or satin facing, with waistcoat and trousers of the same material, the latter plain or with a braid down the sides. The "dress" waistcoat can also be of white duck or piqué, in which case it is double-breasted. The shape of the dress waistcoat shows the shirt bosom in the form of a "U."

The evening shirt is of plain white linen, with two shirt buttons and link cuffs, straight standing collar, white lawn or linen tie. The gloves are white with white stitching, the hose of black silk, and the handkerchief, which must be present but not seen, of plain white linen. The shoes are patent-leather pumps or "low quarters," tied, not buttoned.

The overcoat is an Inverness of black cheviot, lined with satin and without sleeves, and the hat a crush opera. These two latter adjuncts are not indispensable, but most convenient. An ordinary black overcoat and top hat can be worn with evening dress. No visible jewelry—not even a watch chain—is allowed. The shirt buttons are either of white enamel, dull-finished gold, or pearls, and the sleeve links white-enameled or lozenge-shaped disks of gold, with a monogram thereon engraved.

Evening dress is *de rigeur* at balls, dances, evening receptions, evening weddings, dinners, suppers, the opera, and the theater, when calling after candlelight, and in fact at any formal evening function and generally when ladies are present.

INFORMAL EVENING DRESS

Informal evening dress differs from formal in the wearing of the Tuxedo or dinner coat in place of the "swallowtail," and the substitution of a black silk for a white lawn tie.

The dinner coat is of black worsted or vicuña, satin-faced. It is the badge of informality. Formerly it was only worn at the club, at small stag dinners, and on occasions when ladies were not present. Now it is in vogue during the summer at hotel hops and at small informal parties to the play, at bowling parties, restaurant dinners, and, in fact, on any occasion which is not formal. From June to October men wear it in town every evening without overcoat.

As the dinner jacket is short, a top or silk hat can not be worn with it. The proper headgear in winter is a black felt soft hat, in summer a straw.

The dinner jacket is becoming a necessity. It is worn also by all youths and boys from twelve years to seventeen, at which latter period they can assume the *toga virilis* or swallowtail.

ESSENTIAL SARTORIAL TIPS

I here append a few cautionary hints which must be taken if you wish to dress well.

All scarves and ties should be tied by one's self. Made-up neckwear of any kind is not worn by well-groomed men.

White evening waistcoats and Tuxedo coats do not agree; black is only allowable.

Jewelry is vulgar. The ring for a man is a seal of either green or red stone, or of plain burnished gold with the seal or monogram engraved upon it. It must be worn on the little finger.

Watch chains and watch fobs are not in vogue. Watches and latchkeys are attached to a key chain and hidden in the trousers pocket. Diamonds are only in good form when set in a scarf pin, and even then they are in questionable taste. Diamond buttons and diamond rings are absolutely vulgar.

The fashionable overcoat in winter is a Chesterfield or single-breasted frock of kersey or like material in brown, blue, or black, with velvet collar. For autumn and spring the tan covert coat is in vogue.

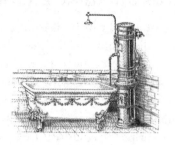

Chapter III

THE BACHELOR'S TOILET

A BACHELOR'S BATHING REGIME

The first care of a bachelor is his bath or tub. To-day, houses—especially clubs and bachelor apartments—are fitted up so luxuriously that each tenant has his own individual tiled bathroom, which he uses also as a dressing room. But where these are not, the tin or the India-rubber bath tub serves as well the purpose of our first ablution. A cold bath to many is a good refresher and awakener, but there are others again whose constitutions can not stand the shock, especially in winter, of icy-cold water. For cleansing purposes, tepid water is best, or a mixture of hot and cold, so as to take the chill off.

A gentleman takes at least one tub a day, and that, as may be inferred from the previous remarks, when he arises. If the tub is in the bedroom, have a rubber cloth placed under, and fill it only half full. The sponge is used for the bath, the wash rag for the washstand. The body should have a thorough soaping. The soap should be either Castile or a pure unscented glycerin. Sweet-scented soaps, perfumery, and sweet waters of all kinds should be eschewed. The Turkish towel is the best for drying, and it should be vigorously but not roughly applied. A flesh brush may be also used with comfort. As soon as the body is perfectly dry the bath robe or large Turkish towel, which some prefer to wrap themselves in, like Indians, should be resumed and shaving begun.

A CLEAN SHAVE

Every man should learn to shave himself. Razors are very delicate instruments and should be kept in thorough order. Safety razors with little blades for each day in the week are excellent, but if you use the ordinary razor add to your collection from time to time, until you have at least half a dozen. Once a month send these to a barber to be stropped, and strop them yourself both before and after using. Wipe them dry with a piece of chamois cloth and put them back in their cases. The best strop is of Russia leather or of canvas.

Warm water is not absolutely necessary for shaving, as some beards are soft and resist heat.

If possible, arrange a shaving stand with a triplicate mirror and places for your razors, shaving mug, brush, and soap. You can purchase one of these, with the entire outfit, for a few dollars at any of the large city shops. A ring or little silver or metal hook for shaving paper can be placed on one side of the stand. A cleanly man shaves every morning. After shaving, wash the face with a little warm water and wipe it thoroughly dry. Add to the water a few drops of ammonia or of Pond's extract, if the skin is liable to chap.

A TIP FROM THE AUTHOR

In the fashion of beards, the clean or smooth-shaven face, the pointed beard, and the simple mustache are those generally in vogue. Should you wear a beard, you should have for it a special comb and brush.

CLEANING ONE'S EYES

A small tin basin, a package of sea salt, and a special wash rag are the requisites for a morning eye bath. Sea salt and warm water are recommended by oculists as the best tonic for the eyes.

DENTAL DUTIES

The teeth next claim your attention. There is nothing more disgusting than foul breath, which comes frequently from neglected teeth. Use a soft toothbrush. Avoid patent tooth washes and lotions.  An excellent tooth powder is made of two thirds French chalk, one third orris root, and a pinch of myrrh. Any chemist will put this up for fifteen cents. Tepid and not cold water should be used. In rinsing the mouth a drop or two of listerine added to the water is excellent. Teeth should be brushed at least twice a day—morning and evening. Never use soap on your toothbrush. Get a spool of dental silk—it will cost you eight cents—and draw the thread between your teeth before you retire, so as to remove any substance which might have got into a crevice. And, above all, have your teeth examined carefully by a good dentist at least twice a year.

See that your toothbrush is sweet and clean, and place it handle down in the tooth mug.

MANICURING HANDS AND FEET

The hands should be well washed and dried, tepid water, scentless soap, and a smooth towel being used. The nails should have a vigorous rubbing with a good nailbrush in the morning before your meals and before you go to bed at night. The nail file and nail scissors must be used as often as possible. Remember, dirty finger nails betray the vulgar and the unkempt. A man with dirty hands is impossible.

The nails should not be pointed, but well rounded and kept free of bits of callous skin around the base, called "hangnails." Finger nails should be kept short, just a bit beyond the fleshy tip of the finger.

The nails of the toes should be kept as carefully as those of the hands. In summer a little talcum powder on the feet will prevent the odor of perspiration.

A GENTLEMAN'S CROWNING GLORY

The fashions for parting the hair change with the times. At present it is the direct part in the middle which is most fashionable. Very young men wear their hair unusually long, but this fad is uncleanly. The hair should be cut at least once a month, and a glimpse of the skin of the neck should always intervene between the roots and the collar.

Pomatums and greases and scents of all kinds are sticky and injurious. If you suffer with dryness of the scalp rub a little vaseline into it occasionally. Washings with tar soap or with a little alcohol and rosemary are beneficial. The scalp should be well brushed with moderately firm but not hard bristles. The best brushes are those without handles, known as army and navy. Water is bad for the hair. Constant combing with a fine-tooth comb is apt to irritate the scalp and provoke dandruff, which can be allayed by brushing, shampooing, and the use of borax and warm water.

A TIP FROM THE AUTHOR

Turkish or Russian baths are beneficial now and then, and the vigorous massage after a thorough steaming is admirable for the skin.

MAINTAINING AN ORDERLY BATHROOM

A man should be scrupulously neat about his toilet articles and appliances. In your bathroom you should have a rack for your coarse and fine towels. Always place the towel you have used at the side of a stationary or on the back of a movable tub to dry. See that the soap is removed from your sponges, and once a fortnight clean them in one quarter of an ounce of borax dissolved in tepid water. Let them soak for an hour, and squeeze them out in clean water.

Hairbrushes are washed in a little soda put into a quart of hot water. The brush must be dipped downward so as not to wet the back. When they are cleansed they can be rinsed in cold water and stood on their side, after the water is shaken out, until quite dry.

Nailbrushes must be turned on their sides, after using, so that the water will not soak in and crack their backs.

A man's toilet articles, whether in silver or wood, should be of one distinctive style and material. Tooth and nail brushes should never have silver handles, but hair and clothes brushes with silver backs are very smart. They should be kept polished with a chamois cloth, and occasionally a little silver polish or whiting. Your bureau or dressing table is the place for the hair and clothes brushes, the combs, the toilet mirror, nail files, nail scissors, and such smaller articles. Your nail and tooth brushes and soaps go on the wash-hand stand. Your sponges are best put in a little wire basket at the side of the wash-hand stand, or the immovable washstand if your room or bathroom has the latter convenience.

A LAST WORD

Your bedroom should be ventilated and all the windows opened after you leave it, and you should have at least one window up during your sleeping hours. If you have a movable tub see that it is aired each morning after using.

Always make a change of clothes and of shoes when you come in from a busy day and from the street. Nothing ruins clothes so much as lounging about your room in them. And last but not least, as it contains the essential of all these rules and hints, be always immaculately clean.

Chapter IV

THE CARE OF A BACHELOR'S CLOTHES

CARE OF PRODUCT

There are comparatively few men who can afford the luxury of a good valet, and that personage himself, when found thoroughly competent, is indeed a treasure. But it is an absurd mistake for any one to think that a valet is a necessity. If you take a quarter of an hour for the care of your clothes every day, you can be just as well turned out as if you hired an expensive servant. Even if you have indulged in the luxury of a valet, you yourself should know all about looking after your wardrobe.

HANDLING YOUR CLOTHES

Whenever you change your clothes you should first empty all your pockets. Then, as soon as each garment is removed, it should be vigorously shaken and brushed before it is folded and put away. Never hang coats, trousers, or waistcoats; always fold them. Wire coat hangers and trousers stretchers ruin clothes. Whisk brooms are useful only when an extra-vigorous treatment is desired. Take a clothes brush and give your coat, as soon as you take it off, a thorough brushing, and hold it to the light, so that no particle of dust may escape your eye. The coat is then folded exactly in half lengthwise, sleeve to sleeve, the lining on the outside. With evening coats it is sometimes necessary to fold the sleeves in half, owing to the shortness of the waist. In packing a trunk the same method is used, only the sleeves are stuffed with tissue paper to avoid possible wrinkles.

Large and bulky garments, such as overcoats and frock coats, should be folded in triplicate. Lay the coat flat on a table and first fold on both sides, the right and the left, so much of the lapel and collar lengthwise as will cover the sleeve. This will make two folds from the top of the collar to the bottom of the skirt. Then fold the coat again in half lengthwise, using the back as a hinge. You will find the same principle illustrated by a cook with a pancake. The waistcoat is folded in half, with the lining on the outside. Always take off your shoes and unbutton the braces before you remove your trousers, and fold them over the back of a chair, which is to serve you as a clothes rack. Take the trousers by the waist and place together the first two suspender buttons, one on the left and the other on the right. This will make the fold preserve the natural crease and dispose of the extra material, button and buttonhole tab at the waist. Trousers carefully folded will only need pressing about twice a year. Hose should be well shaken, and unless perfectly clean, thrown in the soiled-linen basket. Evening silk hose can be worn several times. The undervest, or undershirt, and the drawers should be also subjected to a vigorous shaking, and hung on the back of the same chair where you have already placed your hose. All these intimate garments are to be aired, and the chair on which you have hung them taken to the window.

STORING YOUR CLOTHES

Use a closet and a chest of drawers for your clothes. If you are in very limited quarters, six drawers and a trunk should be sufficient for all your belongings.  The evening clothes occupy one drawer or shelf, and the morning and afternoon suits the other or two others. The remainder will be for linen, underclothing, ties, and handkerchiefs.

Between each suit of clothes there should be laid a newspaper; those publications which use the blackest of printer's ink—the surest antidote for moths—being the best for this purpose. Cover the top of each pile of clothes, when the drawer or shelf is full, with a clean towel.

In a chest with four drawers the bottom one should be used for underclothes, the top for handkerchiefs, hose, and ties, and the two intermediate for your linen. The closet will have to serve for your suits of clothes, or, in lieu of that, your trunk. Otherwise the last-mentioned receptacle is the place for clothes out of season, carefully laid away with a full complement of newspaper and camphor.

When you remove your shirt at night, or when you change for dinner, be careful to take out the buttons and sleeve links, unless you intend to wear the garment again. In that case, hang it up in your closet.

KEEPING YOUR HANDKERCHIEFS HANDY

The first gift which a bachelor usually receives from his sister or his sweetheart is a handkerchief case, and I hardly need advise you to purchase what is a standard Christmas offering. Keep your handkerchiefs in this, your neatly folded ties in the second division of the drawer, and your hose in the third. If you should have a silver and plush pincushion with a movable top, your small articles of jewelry go in its interior, or in a small box in the top drawer.

A HAT FOR EVERY OCCASION

Silk hats, Derbies, and Alpines or soft-felt hats should never be brushed with a whisk broom. A hatter will sell you for a small sum a soft brush with a pliable plush back, which will do for smoothing your silk hat, the bristles to be applied in removing the dust. A silk handkerchief will also smooth a silk hat. Frequent ironing destroys the nap. Straw hats can be cleaned by first rubbing them over with the half of a lemon, then taking an old nail brush and some brown soap and water and giving it a vigorous brushing. Then you should take heavy books and lay them on the brim of the hat. An old pincushion or several towels rolled into a firm ball, or a book which will fit exactly, should be placed inside the crown. Allow the hat to dry, and do not remove the weights until this is accomplished. You will find your straw as good as new and the shape preserved. The writer has tried this with great success.

SHAPING AND SHINING YOUR SHOES

Boots and shoes when not in use should be put on wooden trees to keep them in shape. As trees are rather expensive, one can use paper and stuff it inside the boot or shoe. This will not prove a bad substitute. With patent leathers, paper or cotton stuffed in the toes prevents the leather from wrinkling, and in this instance the very cheap material is better than the more expensive appliance. Patent leathers must be creamed and rubbed with a chamois cloth or linen or flannel rag after all mud and dust have first been removed. This operation should be repeated daily. Some men maintain that patent leathers should be varnished as soon as they come home from the bootmaker, but I disagree with them. A varnished patent leather has always a cheap look, and the coat of veneer is only applied as a last resort, to hide the cracks. Russet boots and shoes are treated daily with the special cream sold for them, which can be obtained at any bootmaker's or shoe shop. The price is small, and the stuff will last a long time. Russet boots, however, can be very well treated with a little vaseline, but that product will not give them the deep-brown color which is so fashionable. The soles of boots and shoes should be painted black. When a man is obliged to kneel in any ceremony, the sight of white or yellow gleaming soles is absurd.

A TIP FROM THE AUTHOR

In wet weather it is absolutely necessary to turn up
the bottoms of your trousers, to keep them
from fraying.

A MONTHLY CLEAN

I would suggest a general overhauling of clothes about
once a month. At the end of each season the heavy or light
garments should receive a final brushing and be stored
away in a trunk, chest, or spare room with, as I have already
advised, newspapers between them, and some camphor or
moth destroyer as an extra precaution. Overcoats, which
are in such general use, may be hung during their season of
service, but should be frequently brushed and well shaken.

PACKING YOUR BAGS

The economy of space thus observed in the arrangement
of clothes in a room will make it an easy matter when
about to travel to pack one's wardrobe in a trunk.

A shoe bag is a great convenience. A simple canvas
arrangement can be purchased very cheaply, or one of
your fair friends can make you one. Your shoes should
be placed in this and put at the bottom of the trunk in a
corner. Otherwise you should wrap your shoes and boots
in paper. If you travel with two trunks, one should be
reserved for your outer garments and the other for your
shirts and underclothes. With one trunk, a shirt box is

as much an article to be desired as a shoe bag, but in lieu of this the shirts should be placed in the first or top tray, the underclothes and hose in the second, and the outer garments in the bottom. A small space in the top can be reserved for your ties and handkerchiefs. Toilet articles are carried in a hand bag; waterproofs, overcoats, and umbrellas and walking sticks in a shawl strap. Your silk hat has but one place, and that is in a hatbox. You can put a Derby in a corner of a trunk but a silk hat would be ruined.

When a long journey is taken, it is economy in the end to purchase an extra steamer trunk for your underclothes and linen. Trunks are not expensive, and you will find that by not crowding your clothes you will save in the long run.

AT HOME AND AT WORK

Never lounge around your room in your street or evening dress. If you are to stay awhile, or if you come in for the night, take off your clothes and put on a bath robe or your pyjamas if you do not possess a dressing gown, which is not a necessity.

At your office you should always have an old coat to wear, and if it be summer have one of linen. To sit around in one's shirt sleeves, even at one's place of business, is not characteristic of the gentleman.

THE COST OF CLOTHES

Every young man starting in life and wishing naturally to take a part in social functions and to become a member of that body indefinitely known as society, is confronted with the problem of clothes. A few years ago the ordinary changes of morning, afternoon, and evening were all that were requisite, but to-day, with special  costumes for various sports and pastimes, the outlook at first glance to one of limited income is not encouraging. And yet a man with a modest salary can dress very well on two to three hundred dollars a year, and even less. It is only the first step which costs. One must have a foundation or a slight capital with which to start. After that with a little care expenses can be easily regulated.

The evening suit is the most expensive essential of a man's wardrobe. This he is obliged to have. I would advise, in selecting a suit of this kind, to have it of good material from a good tailor, after a model not too pronounced, so that in case of any small alteration in the fashions it can survive a season or two. With proper care your evening suit should last at least five years. During the first two or three it should be your costume for formal occasions. During the third season you might possibly have another pair of trousers made or renew the waistcoat or even the coat. When you find yourself, thus by the principles of the doctrine of the survival of the fittest, the possessor of two evening suits, use the old one for theaters and small dinners, and the best for the formal functions. White waistcoats are very smart for evening wear, and an investment in one or two of these during the course of a season will save the waistcoat of the evening suit. The prices of evening suits vary. The most fashionable Fifth Avenue tailors charge as much as one hundred and twenty-five dollars for them. Some men argue that this sum insures an excellent investment. However, you can have an excellent one made by a good tailor for an outlay of about forty dollars. The large retail clothing shops have a custom department, and that is their figure for an evening suit made to order. You can even have one for twenty-five dollars, but I would not spend a less amount. Superintend the making of it yourself. Some men have adjustable figures, and they can purchase their clothes from the block—that is, ready-made. The only fault to find with these garments is their machinelike cut. The pockets, if any, the lines, the binding, and the entire get-up look as if these affairs had been turned out by the dozen.

White waistcoats for evening wear are, however, somewhat in the nature of luxuries. They are difficult to have laundered, and some very smart men object to having them sent to the wash, and would not wear one after it has gone through that process. It may fit you perfectly, but yet again it may not look a whit better than the ready-made which you can purchase at a haberdasher's for from three to five dollars.

A Tuxedo or dinner coat, as explained in another chapter, is almost a necessity. It is really a saving. If you can not afford to have an entire suit of this kind made you may simply have the jacket, which will cost from twenty-five to forty dollars, and wear it with the trousers and waistcoat, and keep it to be part of your informal evening dress.

I have known men to have their black sack coats or old black diagonal cutaways or old evening coat changed into a Tuxedo by the cutting off of tails, the substitution of a silk collar, or some other alteration. A sack coat is easily arranged, and any little tailor around the corner will make the metamorphosis for three dollars. Suppose you have had one of your old coats transformed into a Tuxedo. You can purchase, if you do not wish to have made, a pair of black trousers of the same material for a very few dollars, and an old black waistcoat, which went with the original coat, can also be altered. Remember that a Tuxedo dinner coat has not to be of a certain material. It must be black and have a silk collar. It is really *negligé*.

You should start with a capital of at least six evening shirts. If you are a wealthy man these will cost possibly, made to order, as high as fifty-six dollars, but you can also have excellent ones for nine dollars. It is considered smart to have the collars attached, but not necessary. The cuffs, however, should be always a part of the shirt.

White ties are twenty-five to thirty-five cents a piece. Always state the number of collar you wear when purchasing evening ties, and you will never have cause to complain of the length.

Black patent-leather pumps, made to order, are from eight to nine dollars. You can get them much cheaper ready made, but the only trouble with them is that they are not usually good fits, and that in future years you will have cause to regret this economy. Of black silk stockings, of which you will need two or three pairs, you can have a choice from a dollar and a half to six dollars a pair.

WARDROBE NECESSITIES

I would advise the purchase of two business or lounge suits a year for the first three years. In making this estimate I can hardly suppose that you are in the state of Adam, and I would advise you to wear your old suit in winter especially, and on rainy and stormy days. Your overcoat will conceal it in the street, and at the office the older the clothes the better. The pivotal points of a man are his hat, boots, and tie. Have these perfectly correct, and the rest will take care of itself.

For winter buy a thick, useful cloth, such as Scotch homespun or rough cheviot or tweed. Brown and gray mixtures are always fashionable and wear well.

In summer a light-gray check or a blue cheviot or flannel are always smart.

Thus making an old suit of the year before alternate with the new one, you will find that eighty dollars will be sufficient to help you be a well-groomed man.

A half dozen colored shirts for morning wear are necessary, with attached cuffs but detached collars. Every now and then I would invest a few dollars in shirts, and before you know it you will have a large supply. As dress shirts grow old send them to be repaired at any of the many places which you will find advertised, and use them for morning shirts.

Six changes of underwear—merino or wool—and a dozen balbriggan or woolen hose will be sufficient. Summer underwear is very cheap, and you can get a light merino suit for one dollar. A four-dollar investment will last several seasons. Good winter underwear is expensive, costing four or five dollars a suit.

Pyjamas of Madras or pongee silk, very effective and pretty, can be had for a dollar and a half to three dollars a suit. Four suits of these—two for summer and two for winter—will last at least two years.

A man must have, besides his dancing pumps, a pair of patent-leather walking boots and a pair of stout common boots for everyday wear. If you can afford it, have two pairs of boots made at the same time, or even more. An investment of fifty dollars in boots, at say eight dollars a pair, would be excellent. You can change daily, and they will last you over a period of two or three or more years.

OPTIONAL GARMENTS

The afternoon suit is more or less a luxury. Unless you frequent afternoon teas or make many afternoon calls, or act as an usher at weddings in any city but New York, the frock coat is not, for the first three or four years of your career, an absolute necessity. In New York, however, where calls are only made in the afternoon, it must form a part of your wardrobe.

A frock coat can be made for forty or fifty dollars; seventy-five to one hundred dollars is charged by the most expensive tailors. When you order it, see that it is not in the extreme of fashion. The conservative garment will last a number of years. The material, as I have already suggested in another chapter, must be of rough worsted, vicuña, or material of that kind, and never of broadcloth.

With it you must have a pair of "fancy" or cashmere trousers. These will cost from eight to fifteen dollars, and they will last you several years. In fact, the purchasing of the afternoon suit in one way is excellent: it does not have to be renewed as often as other parts of your wardrobe. It stays practically in fashion, with little deviation, for almost a decade.

The silk hat, which is necessary for the afternoon suit, is one of the most expensive items of a man's wardrobe. A top hat must be of the prevailing mode. Autumn is the best time for purchasing, as you can dispense with it after May, except on very special occasions. Two Derbies— one for autumn and the other for spring—at from two to four dollars, or only one, for that matter, to last through the entire eight months, and a straw hat, from two to four dollars, will be the entire amount expended for headgear by the very best-dressed men. For a Derby you can substitute an Alpine or Hombourg. The opera crush hat is a luxury, and you can wear with your evening suit your top hat of the year before, which you can christen your "night hawk."

Shirt buttons and sleeve links are also an expensive item. However, the purchase of these occurs but once in a lifetime, and fifteen dollars would do beautifully for enamel or plain gold.

Ties vary in price, and it is difficult to limit a man on this expenditure. Many invest in them as a fad, picking them up here and there, and thus accumulating a large assortment. A little judgment in purchasing will allow you to acquire quite a large wardrobe. If you give your personal supervision to the making of your clothes you can employ a cheap tailor who will turn out very good work. For fashion plates, I do not know of any better than Du Maurier's pictures of smart London men in the London *Punch*. Watch the sales in the autumn and the late spring for bargains in haberdashery. Study well the advice given in the chapter on the Care of Clothes in this book, and you will find therein that which will certainly teach you economy.

Chapter V

INTRODUCTIONS, INVITATIONS, AND CALLS

INTRODUCTIONS

Formal introductions are not in vogue in this country. The nearest approach to it is when one is desirous of introducing a stranger or one of his particular friends to another. When you desire to present a man to a woman you must ask her if you may bring Mr. —— to her house. In introducing men to one another it is unnecessary to make a formal appointment. In presenting a man to a woman her permission must first be asked. The formula is, "Mrs. C——, may I present Mr. D——?" Informal introductions may be made between people visiting in the same house by simply saying, "Mrs. D——, may I present Mr. B——?" or "Mr. F——, do you know Mr. C——?" These informal introductions need not be recognized afterward unless mutually agreeable.

Introductions are never made in the street or in public places of any kind, or in public conveyances, unless under exceptional circumstances. It is extremely bad form to introduce a guest on his entrance into a room to more than one other. General introductions are not made at a dinner or at any function. People are sufficiently well bred to engage in general conversation when in the houses of their friends, even if they do not know each other, and not to take advantage of the circumstances afterward.

SHAKING HANDS WITH THE FAIRER SEX

A man never shakes hands upon being presented to a woman, but always on being introduced to a man. A man should never shake hands with a woman while wearing his gloves unless she also is gloved. Your hostess will give her hand to you when you make your obeisance. After being presented, an invitation is apt to follow. It may be, "Drop in to tea any afternoon," or simply, "I would be glad to have you call." This invitation should always come from a married woman. Unmarried women do not ask young men to call. A man may ask the privilege of calling, or the mother of the young woman may say, "We should be pleased to have you call, Mr. Smith."

CALLING ON A LADY

In New York and in many of the larger cities, the proper time for a man to call on a woman is between the hours of four and six in the afternoon. Sometimes women have "days" in the season, and you should pay your call on one of them. Otherwise any afternoon may do, and you can use Sunday for this purpose after three o'clock.

Afternoon dress is, of course, requisite. In those places where evening calls are made a man must wear formal evening dress.

On the opening of the door by the servant, a man asks of him whether the hostess or "the ladies" are at home. This will depend on the number of the members of the family receiving. He gives to the domestic the proper number of cards. The servant precedes him, opens the drawing-room door for him, and in some ultra English houses he is announced. His card or cards have been deposited on the silver tray which the servant has presented to him in the hall and left there. A visiting card is never brought into the drawing room. A man on a first or a formal call carries his stick and hat into the drawing room with him. To "hang his hat" in the hall shows great intimacy—even relationship—in the house. He, however, should leave there his overcoat and his rubbers and umbrella. His hostess will advance to meet him, and will extend to him her right hand with a somewhat stiff angular motion, and he should shake it with a quick nervous movement of his right. A man removes his glove from his right hand on entering the drawing room, and holds this with his stick and hat in his left. The hat should be at an angle, the top about level with his nose.

HANDSHAKES FOR DIFFERENT OCCASIONS

At weddings, the opera, and dances, where a woman is gloved, a man, if it is required to shake hands, does not remove his gloves. On ordinary occasions a woman is seldom gloved in her own drawing room, and if she is, handshaking is not usually expected. Should the hostess be gloved, as at a large affair, such as a formal or wedding reception, a man shakes hands with her with them on.

MANNERS AT TEATIME

Tea is generally served in the afternoon on a tray with wafers, little cakes, and sometimes sandwiches. If you

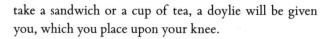

take a sandwich or a cup of tea, a doylie will be given you, which you place upon your knee.

KNOWING WHEN YOUR STAY IS OVER

When another caller enters the room stand up, whether it is a woman or a man. Ten minutes is all that is necessary for a formal call. It is less awkward to leave when a new caller is announced. Shake hands with your hostess and bow to the people present. Leave the room sideways, so as not to turn your back upon the company, and bow to them as you reach the door, thus bowing yourself out. Remember, do not be a lingerer or a sitter. No men are more dreaded in society than these wretched bores. The first arrivals leave first. Freezing out is not known in good society.

ARRANGING A CALL

Calls should be made after every civility extended and every invitation accepted or regretted; after weddings, wedding receptions, deaths in families, etc., as fully explained in the chapter on card-leaving.

A letter of introduction is always sent, never left in person. Calls at the theater or in opera boxes are mere social amenities, and are not accepted as formal. A man enters an opera box, stands, and bows. His hostess will turn around and greet him. He will then, if there is a vacant chair, take one, and sit and talk a little while, leaving on the arrival of another caller. These rules for afternoon calls can be applied also to those made in the evening.

If no day is set for a first call, a man is expected to drop in any afternoon within ten days after the invitation. The sooner a call is made the greater the compliment. A second call may be made within two or three months; after that once or twice a year, as intimacy permits. A man is never asked to dinner or to any function at a house at which he has not first called.

EXAMPLES OF INVITATIONS AND R. S. V. P.s

The usual form of a dinner invitation, the hostess being married, reads:

> *My dear Mr. Smith:*
> *Will you dine with us, most informally, on Wednesday, December the ninth, at eight o'clock? Hoping that you have no engagement for that evening, believe me,*
> *Yours very sincerely,*
> *Alice de Tompkins.*
> *November thirtieth.*

An answer to an invitation like this, which should be sent within twenty-four hours, reads:

> *My dear Mrs. de Tompkins:*
> *It will give me great pleasure to dine with you on Wednesday evening, December the ninth, at eight o'clock. With many thanks for your kind thought of me,*
> *Yours very sincerely,*
> *Algernon Smith.*
> *December first.*

Or, in the case of a formal dinner consisting of more than ten or twelve guests:

> *Mr. and Mrs. de Tompkins*
> *request the pleasure of*
> *Mr. Smith's*
> *company at dinner on*
> *Wednesday evening, December*
> *the ninth, at eight o'clock.*

The answer reads:

> *Mr. Algernon Smith, Jr.,*
> *accepts with pleasure*
> *Mr. and Mrs. de Tompkins's*
> *kind invitation for*
> *Wednesday evening, December the ninth,*
> *at eight o'clock.*
> *December first.*

Answers to formal luncheon invitations are written in the same manner, only changing the hours, etc.

Informal invitations to breakfasts and luncheons will be treated in the chapter on that subject.

The form of an invitation to a private dance is:

> *Mr. and Mrs. de Tompkins request the pleasure of Mr.*
> *Algernon Smith's company on Friday evening, January the*
> *ninth, at nine o'clock.*
> *R. S. V. P. Dancing.*

The answer to this would be similarly worded as in case of the formal dinner. As dance invitations are usually sent out three weeks in advance, three days' grace is allowed for the answer.

When an invitation is received to a subscription ball, like the assemblies in various cities, you should acknowledge it, by your acceptance or regret, to the subscriber sending it; but when an invitation is received from a ball committee, you should accept as follows:

Mr. James de Courcy Peterson accepts with pleasure the committee's kind invitation for Thursday evening, February the fifteenth.
January second.

Chapter VI

CARDS

ONLY THE BEST WILL DO

There is only one visiting card in vogue for a man. It must be of plain white bristol board, unglazed, about three or four inches in length and about two inches in width. The name should be engraved, not printed, in the middle of the card, in small copperplate type, without ornamentation of any kind.

WHAT'S IN A NAME?

The prefix "Mr." is always used unless the person is a physician, in which case he can place "Dr." before his name, or a clergyman, when he may use the "Rev. Mr." or the "Rev. Dr.," according to his rank. Army and navy men, ranking as captain or above, should put their rank on their cards. "Mr." is the prefix for subalterns. The address is placed underneath the name in smaller type and in the right-hand corner. If an address, however, is that of a man's club, it should be engraved on the left hand. A man's card should also contain his Christian as well as his surname. If he possesses two Christian names, or any distinctive family name, that should also be given, so that his appellation is shown in full. For instance, "Mr. John William Jones," "Mr. James Brown Smith," "Mr. Hamilton Hamilton-Stuyvesant."

CARRYING YOUR CARDS

Visiting cards should be kept in a small case of sealskin or black or Russia leather and carried in the inside pocket of a frock coat, or if small enough more conveniently in the waistcoat pocket. Card cases should be stamped with initials or have a silver monogram. Visiting cards should never be carried loose in the pocket.

CONTACTING BY CARD

A card is left in person the day after a dinner, luncheon, or breakfast, or within a week at latest after a ball. Civility must be returned by civility, and cards must be left on every occasion on which a call is necessary. Cards should not be sent by mail, unless when about to leave the country, or under circumstances where it is impossible to make a personal call. On leaving the country you should write the initials P. P. C. (*pour prendre congé*) in the right-hand corner.

HOW MANY CARDS IS TOO MANY?

The question of how many cards to leave is one which seems to bewilder most people. The general rule is a card to each person. This will have to be explained. When you call on Mr. and Mrs. Smith you must leave a card for each—two cards. When you call on Mr. and Mrs. Smith and the Misses Smith, three cards, the young ladies counting as a unit. For Mr. and Mrs. Smith, the Misses Smith, and their married daughter Mrs. Jones staying with them, four cards—Mrs. Jones being entitled to the fourth. If Mr. Jones is also stopping at the Smiths leave an extra card for him. For Mrs. Smith (widow) and the Misses Smith, two cards. For Mr. Smith (widower) and the Misses Smith, two cards.

ADDRESS TO IMPRESS

In mailing cards, address them on the envelope "Mrs. Smith, the Misses Smith," or "Mr. and Mrs. John Brown-Smith"; "The Misses Brown-Smith," the one under the other. Never write on your cards "For Mr. and Mrs. John Brown-Smith." It is bad form. Never leave cards for people who have not asked you to call. When friends from another city, who have entertained you or who have been polite to you, should arrive in your own city, you should immediately call and leave cards for them. In that case, should you even not be acquainted with their host and hostess, it would be civil to leave cards also for them.

CARDS FOR THE BRIDE AND GROOM

After a wedding, if invited to the reception, you must personally leave cards at the house where the reception has been given for your host and hostess, and also for the young couple when they return from their bridal trip. Two cards at each place will be sufficient in this case. When invited to the church only, leave or send cards to the bride's parents and the young couple. As the card to the church only, is rather an equivocal compliment, mailing cards in this case could be excused.

CARDS FOR MISCELLANEOUS OCCASIONS

Leave personally cards for the patroness who has asked you to a subscription ball, within a week after the invitation.

In cases of death, leave cards within a fortnight. In answer to letters of condolence, it is best to send your cards with the words "Thank you for your kind sympathy" written thereon. For mourning, use the same size or style of card, but with a narrow or deep border as befits the nearness of degree of relationship with the deceased. The deepest border permissible is about a quarter of an inch. It is bad form to bend cards or to turn down the corners thereof. These signs mean nothing now in good society.

DELIVERING A CARD

In calling—it may be repeated here—you ask, if there are more than one of the fair sex in the house, for "the ladies," and hand the servant the number of cards necessary. He takes them on a silver salver and leaves them in the hall, goes before you, and announces you. Your card is never taken to the lady of the house, unless it is a business call.

Chapter VII

THE DINER-OUT

DEFINITION OF THE "DINER-OUT"

When I speak of the "diner-out," I include under this title the bachelor guest not only at dinners, but also at luncheons and at suppers. The formal breakfast is a festivity of the past, and the first meal in a household is purely a family affair. However, luncheons on Sunday at one or two o'clock are in New York frequently called breakfasts, because I believe many fashionable people do not want the impression to go abroad that even once a week they dine in the middle of the day. The luncheon after a day wedding ceremony is also called a breakfast, but this, like the Sunday meal, is simply a title by courtesy.

BEING PUNCTUAL

All guests are expected to be punctual to the minute and to take advantage even of the quarter of an hour latitude is bad form. Better a little too early than too late. However, do not make yourself ridiculous by appearing on the scene too soon. Bear in mind that the reputation of being the "late Mr. Smith" is not enviable. A tardy guest only accentuates his own insignificance. This rule applies to dinners and suppers and to all entertainments where you are a guest, with only one exception—dances, where you have an hour's grace.

ATTENDING LUNCHEONS

Luncheons, as a rule, are informal affairs. Men have attended them in lounge suits, but it is more courteous to your hostess to appear in afternoon dress. Overcoats, hats, and sticks are left in the hall. Your gloves are removed in the drawing room. When luncheon is announced, unless it is a very formal affair, your hostess leads the way to the dining room, and she is followed by her guests, women and men, not in procession. The men, of course, must allow the fairer sex to pass before them through the drawing-room door and into the dining room. Luncheon *menus* consist of oysters, clams, or grape fruit with crushed ice and saturated with maraschino for the first course. This is followed by bouillon, an *entrée*, a roast or chops with peas, or broiled chicken, salad with birds, ices and fruits, coffee and *liqueurs*. Sherry and claret are the wines, and sometimes champagne is served.

A luncheon lasts three hours at most, and the men are left to smoke at dessert. However, sometimes this formality is waived.

A TIP FROM THE AUTHOR

Luncheons, where men are guests, are popular entertainments at all the large summer resorts. The hour for a luncheon is half past one o'clock, and sometimes it is advanced to two.

FORMAL DINNERS

Dinner invitations are sent out at least a fortnight in advance. They must, under all circumstances, be answered within twenty-four hours, and cards left on your prospective host and hostess within a week.

The fashionable hours for dining are between half past seven and eight o'clock. Dinners being formal evening functions, formal evening dress is essential.

Except at very small houses and apartments, two rooms are reserved—one for the men and the other for the ladies—as dressing rooms. Your hat, coat, and outdoor attire are removed, and a servant will assist you in arranging your toilet.

The servant who announces you, hands you a small envelope on which is written your name. This incloses a card on which is the name of the lady whom you are to take in to dinner. After exchanging greetings with your hostess and removing your gloves, you should endeavor to find your partner and engage in some preliminary conversation. Should you not have been presented to her, inform your hostess of this fact, and you will be at once introduced. Dinner is announced by the butler entering the drawing room and saying, "Dinner is served." The host leads the way with the woman guest of honor, and you are assigned your place in the procession by the hostess, who comes last with the man guest of honor. Each man offers his right arm to his fair partner. In the dining room, cards are placed at each cover with the names of the guests inscribed thereon. Even should there be a retinue of servants, pull back the chair of your partner and assist her to seat herself. In some old-fashioned houses grace is said, and it is always the rule when a clergyman is one of the guests. This blessing is asked after the company is seated.

During dinner you must devote yourself to the comfort and entertainment of the woman whom you have taken in. She must be your first care, although there may be some one on your other side, or opposite, who is more congenial to you. Talking across the table is very bad form. Let your conversation be pleasant and general, but avoid politics, religion, and personal criticisms.

There is no form for refusing wine, if it is against your scruples to drink it. Do not thus force your personal prejudices on your host by making any demonstration, such as putting your finger over the glass or shaking your head at the butler. Let him fill your glasses, but do not drink the contents. The question of waste is not to be considered; and if you are a man with firm principles regarding total abstinence, in your heart you should rejoice that at least a quota of the fluid will do no harm.

The hostess gives the signal at dessert for the ladies to retire to the drawing room. Everybody rises, and the ladies leave the table in solemn procession, the man nearest the door opening it for them. A prettier custom, and one much in vogue in New York, is the escorting of the ladies by the men to the drawing room, the host leading the way. When the drawing-room door is reached the men bow and retire again to the dining room, where coffee, *liqueurs*, and cigars are served. At the end of a half hour they return to the drawing room. Another half hour of conversation, during which sometimes there is dancing, and the guests make their adieus to their hostess and host and leave. On bidding good-night, always assure your hostess of the pleasant evening which you have enjoyed.

OTHER FORMS OF DINNER PARTY

Progressive dinners are sometimes given, although now almost obsolete. Small tables are arranged for these with parties of four or six at each table. The guests change places at each course, the signal for this being given by the hostess ringing a bell. The ladies remain in their seats. As there will not be a fresh napkin provided at each course, a man brings his with him from his first table.

Public dinners, except when given by certain church, debating, or literary societies, are stag affairs. The guests assemble at the restaurant, hotel, or hall where the banquet is to be held, and deposit their hats, coats, and walking paraphernalia in the cloakroom. A ticket is given with the number of your rack upon it, and a small fee—usually twenty-five cents—is expected. The guests assemble in one of the smaller drawing rooms, and each one is handed a plan of the tables with the location of his cover designated by his name upon it. A procession is formed, the guests of honor and reception committee leading, to the banquet hall. After dessert, speeches are in order.

Dinner dances are a form of entertainment where dinner is followed by a dance, other guests coming in from other dinner parties and meeting at one house which has been agreed upon as the place where the dance is to take place. A short time after dinner, at each of the other houses, the guests are conveyed therefrom in carriages, or, better yet, in stages, to the general rendezvous. Calls are due within the week at the house where you have dined as well as at the one at which you have danced.

SUPPER

Supper etiquette differs but little from that observed at dinners. The occasion is a bit more informal and the *menu* not so elaborate. The etiquette of ball suppers is treated in the chapter on The Dance, and suppers after the play, at restaurants and clubs, being favorite bachelor entertainments, will be explained in that part of this book reserved for the Bachelor as Host.

Chapter VIII

A CODE
OF TABLE
MANNERS

OFT-FORGOTTEN BASICS

Many of the cautions contained in this chapter will seem elementary in their nature. But one expects in a book of this kind to see the old familiar "don'ts," and their absence would perhaps deter from the usefulness of *The Complete Bachelor*. It is really quite surprising to see how few men have perfect table manners. The American is unfortunately too often in a hurry. He bolts his food. He is a victim of the "quick-lunch" system. Again, a bachelor eating a solitary meal at a club or a restaurant is apt from sheer loneliness to try and dispose of it as rapidly as possible. Drill yourself into eating leisurely. Persons of refinement take only small morsels at a time. One can not be too dainty at table. To attempt to talk while your mouth is full is another vulgarity upon which it is needless to dwell. The French have made us the reproach that we frequently drink while our mouths are in this condition. I fear there is some foundation for this accusation. Wipe your mouth carefully before putting a glass to your lips. Grease stains around the edge of a goblet or wineglass are silent but telltale witnesses of careless habits.

MESSY EATERS

The napkin is an embarrassing article to many men. Its place is on the lap and not tucked into the shirt bosom or festooned around the neck. When one arises from the table, the napkin is thrown carelessly on it, unfolded. The days of napkin rings are over.

Nervous and bashful persons fidget, they do not sit squarely or firmly at table, their chairs are crooked, they play or gesticulate with their  knives and forks, or they beat dismal tattoos with them against their plates. These same timid minds find vent for inspiration in the crumbs of the bread, of which they involuntarily make little figures or small round balls. The economist, another person on the list, plasters his food, taking a bit of potato, a little tomato, and a good-sized square of meat as a foundation, and spreading these tidbits one on the other, prepares of them a delectable poultice which he swallows at a mouthful. I pass over the man who leaves traces of each meal on his shirt or his clothes. Such a being, I have no doubt, would convey food to his mouth with his knife, would blow on his soup, tea, or coffee with the idea of cooling it, or would pour the two latter cheering fluids into a saucer and drink them therefrom.

The caution to keep one's hands above the cloth and one's elbows out of reach of others, also falls under the head of kindergarten classification.

OBSOLETE RITUALS

The ridiculous idea prevailing that one must not eat until others are served has passed away with many old-time fallacies. One commences to eat as soon as served. You need not proceed very actively, but you can take up your fork or spoon, as the case may be, and make at least a feint at it.

Toasts have also fallen into "desuetude" at private dinners. Sometimes you will find an old-fashioned host who will, on touching his glass with his lips, bow to his guests, and they may wait for this signal to sip their wine, but the custom is utterly obsolete in large cities and at formal dinners.

SIGNALLING YOU ARE FINISHED

When you have finished the course, lay your knife and fork side by side on your plate, the prongs of the fork upward. Do not cross them. No whist-like signals are needed to-day to signify that you have had sufficient to eat.

SERVING FOOD AND SECOND HELPINGS

Dinners are generally served *à la Russe*—that is, from the sideboard, and the dishes are passed around by the servants on silver trays. Very large *plats*, such as roasts and fish, are sometimes carried without the trays. On all occasions of ceremony the men servants are gloved.

Carving at table is but little seen except at very informal dinners and in the country, where sometimes the master of the house shows off this old-fashioned accomplishment, especially if he has a dining room in colonial style and wishes to have everything in keeping.

The question of second helpings is therefore not one of moment. The servants pass the viands twice or more around. If a host or hostess serves at table, he or she will ask the guests whether they would like a second helping. It is never demanded.

A BAD HABIT

Except when absolutely necessary the handkerchief should be kept out of sight. It can be used in case there should be some sudden irritation of the skin, but to blow one's nose at table is disgusting.

A CODE OF FOOD CONDUCT

There are yet a few men who go in for the old-fashioned hearty breakfast with beefsteak, buckwheat cakes, and trimmings, but in cities the lighter meal is preferable. All this is, of course, more a matter of environment and hygiene than etiquette. I have compiled a list of certain viands, which society does require should be eaten at a special meal and in only one manner. With this catalogue I will close this chapter.

Breakfast and luncheon dishes

Eggs.—It is much better form to have egg cups than egg glasses for boiled eggs. Cut the top of the egg off with a dexterous blow of a sharp knife and eat it in the shell with a small egg spoon.

Sugar.—Lump sugar if served is always taken with the sugar tongs.

Butter.—Butter is only served at breakfast or luncheon. It is passed around in a silver dish, with a little silver pick with which to spear it. Butter plates—i. e., the small round silver or china affairs—have given place to bread and butter plates, which are of china and are somewhat larger than an ordinary saucer. It is needless to add that butter is never served at dinner.

Radishes.—Radishes appear at luncheon. Put them on your bread and butter plate and eat them with a little salt.

Cantaloupes are served cut in half and filled with ice. They are eaten as a first course, a fork being better to eat them with than a spoon. Salt is the condiment to use with them, but sugar is allowable.

Grape fruit is served as a first course (*vide* chapter Diner-Out) at a late breakfast or luncheon. It is eaten with a spoon.

Dinner

The *menu* of to-day is simple. It consists of oysters or clams, according to season, soup, fish, *entrée*, roast and vegetables, game and salad, ices and dessert. Sorbets or frozen punches are not served, except at public banquets and hotel *table-d'hôtes.*

Oysters or *clams* are placed on the table in plates for the purpose before dinner is announced. They are imbedded in ice and arranged around a half-sliced lemon, which is in the middle of the plate. Oysters or clams are eaten with a fork only. Gourmets say that they should not even be cut with it, and should be swallowed whole. I would not advise any one to try this with large oysters. The oyster fork is the first in the number of the implements placed beside your plate. Condiments, such as pepper and salt, will be passed you. Sauterne is served with oysters.

Oyster cocktails have been in vogue in place of oysters. These are a mixture of the bivalve with Tabasco sauce and vinegar, and they are said to be excellent appetizers. They are eaten with a small fork from cocktail glasses. Bachelors frequently serve them in place of oysters.

Soup.—At large and formal dinners a clear soup is in vogue. Your soup spoon will be on the knife side of your plate. Soup is eaten from the side and not from the end of the spoon. The motion of the hand guiding the spoon is toward and not from you. Take soup in small spoonfuls, and use your napkin in wiping your mouth and mustache after each, especially if the soup is thick or a *purée*. This will avoid the dripping of that liquid from your upper lip. Never after this operation throw your napkin back into your lap with the greasy side toward your clothes, but use the inside of it for this purpose.

Fish is eaten with a silver fish fork. Chasing morsels of fish around your plate with bits of bread is obsolete. Silver fish knives have been put in use, but they are not generally the vogue.

Cucumbers are served
with fish on the same
plate. Little plates or saucers
for cucumbers, vegetables, or salads are bad form.

Sherry is served with fish.

Celery, *olives*, and *salted almonds* are placed on the table
in small dishes. Sometimes the guests are asked to help
themselves, but at formal dinners they are passed around
after the fish. Celery is eaten with the fingers and dipped
in a little salt placed on the tablecloth or on the edge of
your plate. It is also served as an *entrée* raw, the stalks
stuffed with Parmesan cheese. It should then be eaten
with a fork.

Entrées require a fork only. Among these are patties,
rissoles, *croquettes*, and sweetbreads.

Mushrooms are eaten with a fork, and served as a separate
course in lieu of an *entrée*.

Terrapin is served sometimes in little silver saucepans
either as an *entrée* or as fish, and again in a chafing dish,
and sometimes with salad. It is more of a supper than a
dinner plat, and should be eaten with a fork.

Asparagus is eaten, except in the intimate privacy of
your own family circle, with a fork. Cut the points off
with the end of the prongs. The stalk or white part is
not eaten. It is allowable to eat it with your fingers, as I
have said, in private. It is served after the roast as a special
course. One can not drink *champagne* with *asparagus* except
at the risk of a severe headache.

Artichokes are served as a separate course after the
roast. They should be placed in the center of your plate

and the inside tips of the leaves alone eaten. The leaves are removed with the fingers and dipped in salt, *sauce vinaigrette*, or melted butter. The center of the artichoke is called the heart. The hairy part is removed with the fork, and the heart itself, which is deliciously tender, is conveyed to the mouth with the fork.

Champagne is served in small tumblers or claret glasses. The champagne stem glasses are out of fashion. The *dry* may be served from the fish to the close of dinner, but the old rule was to give it with the roast, *claret* with the *entrée*, and *Burgundy* with the game.

Salad is eaten with a fork only. In cutting *game* or *poultry*, the bone of either wing or leg should not be touched with the fingers, but the meat cut close off. It is better to sever the wing at the joint.

Savories, a species of salt fish and cheese sandwich, are served in England hot, about the end of dinner. They should be eaten with a fork. Undressed salad is sometimes served with them, or radishes, butter, and cheese. This is the only occasion when one sees butter on a dinner table, and this at informal dinners. The salad undressed can be eaten with the fingers. At bachelor dinners and at luncheons *cheese* is served with salad. The French soft cheeses are the favorites.

Pastry, *ices*, and *desserts* are eaten with a fork.

Fruit, such as peaches, pears, and apples, are served frequently already pared. When this is the case, finger bowls are dispensed with, but as yet this is not a general rule. Usually at dessert there is placed before you a finger glass and doily and a dessert plate, with the dessert knife and fork on either side. Remove the glass and doily; put it in front of your plate a little to the right. *Fruit* must be pared or peeled with a silver knife.

Strawberries are now served with the stems on, and sugar and cream are passed around and are taken on your dessert plate.

Pineapples are eaten with a fork. A cracker is used for nuts, and silver picks are brought in with the dessert.

Corn on the cob is a favorite at small informal dinners as a separate course. In polite society you must remove the grains of the corn with your fork or your knife and fork, and never eat it off the cob holding the end with your fingers. By holding one end with your napkin, you can plow down the furrow of the grains with your fork, and you will find that they will fall off easily. *Corn* is always served, when given in this style, on a white napkin. You help yourself to the ear with your fingers.

Macaroni and *spaghetti* should only be eaten with a fork. In New Orleans boiled *shrimps* are often served at small dinners. The skins and heads are on, and you remove these with your fingers. After this course finger bowls with orange leaves are passed around, and the perfume of the water will remove the odor of fish from your fingers.

Black coffee is served after dinner. Milk or cream does not accompany it, except in the country, where sometimes a little silver pitcher of cream is placed on the tray. Coffee is drunk from small cups. Coffee and milk are never served during dinner, nor again is iced milk. These are barbarisms. Chartreuse, kümmel, curaçoa, and cognac are the *liqueurs* usually served after dinner.

Claret, in many French families, especially those of the middle class, is placed on the table in decanters. You are expected to help yourself. There are also *carafons* or decanters of water to mix with the wine. The claret decanters are called *carafes*. Claret is drunk at the twelve o'clock *déjeuner* as well as at dinner.

Tea is passed around in old-fashioned English houses about an hour after dinner. In some places buttered muffins accompany it, but this extra refreshment is only seen now in very old-fashioned houses.

Scotch whisky and hot water or mineral waters are served in country houses before bedtime.

Chapter IX

THE CITY BACHELOR AS HOST

THE ADVANTAGES OF HOSTING

The bachelor who entertains is a most popular member of society. It does not cost a fortune to return in some manner the civilities once received, and every man, even if his income be limited, can once in a while entertain, even if it be on a very small scale and in a very modest way. Bachelor functions are always enjoyable. For a host of moderate income, I would suggest a luncheon, a dinner, or a party to the play, followed by a little supper.

ORGANISING A LUNCHEON

A bachelor luncheon can be given either at the host's apartments or chambers, at a restaurant, or in the ladies' annex of his club, if that organization possesses such an institution.

At all entertainments given under a bachelor's vine and fig tree, extreme simplicity should be a characteristic. The table linen should be of the finest damask, or the best material his income will allow; the glass perfectly plain, clear crystal, the china of a rich but quiet pattern, the silver good but absolutely without ornamental devices of any kind. In fact, the silver can be limited to forks and spoons, and the rest Sheffield or prince's plate. Silver is not expensive, but plate is considered quite smart, and it has the advantage of being utterly valueless from the burglar's point of view.

Individual salt and pepper affairs, cut or colored glass, or the hundred and one knick-knacks which one sees advertised and which eventually find their way to the boarding-house table, are vulgar.

LAYING THE TABLE

Before your cloth is laid you should have a cover of felt placed over the table, so as to form a shield between it and the damask or linen. In the center goes a silver or plated fernery, filled with ferns and asparagus vines, on a mirror tray, or an *épergne* with fruit. Two heavy, old-fashioned decanters in Queen Anne coasters should be placed, one at your right and the other at the right of your *vis-à-vis*. These contain sherry  and claret. Four plain silver, plated, or china dishes are at the corners with salted almonds, olives, *bonbons*, and fancy cakes. If you wish to be very effective and have the money to spare, it is smart at a dinner to have silver candlesticks with candles or tiny lamps gleaming behind red or pink shades at each cover. Two or three forks are laid at the left of each plate. If more are required, your servant will replace them. On the right of the plate are the knives, including one for the roast, with the tablespoon for the soup, if it is a dinner, and the oyster fork. The napkins should be plain and flat, and contain a roll of bread. These hints for arranging the table will do for either luncheon or dinner. Not one of the articles is in itself expensive, and you may possess them all with the accumulation of years. If not, a simpler arrangement could be effected, or you could give the entertainment at a restaurant instead of your rooms or house.

INVITING YOUR GUESTS

The invitations can be either verbal or written, but at best a luncheon or dinner in a bachelor's apartments is regarded as a little frolic, and you must try to preserve the spirit and waive the formalities.

WAITING STAFF

A chaperon, of course, is necessary. The party can be limited to about eight. If you have a manservant he should be dressed in black coat and trousers, white shirt, standing collar and tie, and liveried waistcoat. His duties are to open the door and to serve the luncheon. But a manservant is not necessary. Some of the smartest bachelors in New York give delightful little dinners and luncheons at their apartments, at which the maid who has cooked the meal, dressed in white apron and black gown, also serves it.

A QUIET AFFAIR

The *menu* should be the usual one expected at luncheons, but champagne is never offered by a man to women in his apartments, unless at dinner or a theater supper. If a wealthy bachelor has a large house, and instead of one there are a number of matrons chaperoning, the case is different. Manhattan or Martini cocktails could be passed around before luncheon, or some little peculiar dish be served to give a zest to the occasion.

A bachelor's dinner at his house or apartments is a more formal entertainment, but it differs in nowise from a regular function of that character. The chaperon takes the place of the lady of the house for that occasion. Dressing rooms are arranged for the men and women, and the same ceremonies observed as at any formal dinner. If the affair is given in apartments, of course the character must be more or less informal, as the accommodations are limited. Should you have a man serve at your dinner, he must be in evening dress. Both at dinner and at luncheon he must have gloves, but this is not required of a maid.

A bachelor's supper in his own apartments is sometimes given after the play. Of the *menu*, I will speak a little farther on. A chafing-dish supper is, however, an unique and enjoyable entertainment. Several chafing dishes should be ready, so that each course can follow without delay. Terrapin, truffled eggs, curried oysters, and other dainties of this kind comprise usually the *menu*. It would be well to serve first oysters on the half shell, followed by lobster *à la Newburg*, the latter being the first *plat* cooked with the chafing dish. Champagne is a good wine, and allowable for a chafing-dish supper; but if Welsh rarebits are the *chef d'œuvre*, then beer or ale would be better.

THEATER OUTINGS

A theater party should be confined to eight or ten. A *parti carré*—four people—is delightful. Unmarried women do not go to theaters or restaurants with a man alone. They must be chaperoned, even at  a matinée or a luncheon party at a hotel or restaurant—in fact, an unmarried couple is seldom seen at public places, unless they are engaged, and married women are as much compromised as unmarried ones by indifference to this absolute rule of etiquette.

The invitations can be either verbal or written. In the season it is better to write them, to insure the acceptance of guests. Be careful in the wording to give not only the evening, but the name of the play and the theater. For a party, always secure end seats, and there will be no disturbing of others in case you might be a little late. A box is necessary at the circus or at a music hall, but orchestra seats or stalls are the best selection for a bachelor's party. Many mothers object to their daughters being seen at the theater in a proscenium box.

The rendezvous or meeting place should be at the chaperon's. The vestibule of the theater is awkward, except for parties of four. A stage is the best vehicle to convey your guests to the playhouse. At the theater the host sees that his guests are provided with playbills. He gives the tickets to the usher, and precedes the party down the aisle. He indicates the order of sitting. A man should go in first, followed by the woman with whom he is to sit, and then, thus sandwiched, the rest of the party file in, the host taking the aisle or end seat. The host sits next to the chaperon. Gentlemen do not go out between the acts at the theater, but sometimes, when there is a party to the opera, they can leave their seats if other men come to visit the ladies. A man going in or out a theater aisle should do so with his face toward the stage and his back to the seat. A host never leaves his guests. After the play go a little ahead and give your carriage check to the porter as soon as possible, so that there may not be a long wait. The porter expects a small fee. All theater parties are followed by a supper given either at a restaurant, at the club, in the ladies' annex, or at your bachelor apartments.

HOSTING RESTAURANT ENGAGEMENTS

All luncheons, dinners, or suppers at a restaurant, unless organized on the spur of the moment, are ordered beforehand, and everything, including the waiter's tip, arranged and settled for. If you have not an account at the restaurant, pay the bill at the time you order the *menu* and reserve the table. Flowers should be included, and a centerpiece of roses, which are so arranged as to come apart and be distributed in bunches to each of your fair guests, is one of the favorite devices. Small *boutonnières* are provided for the men. The public restaurant or dining room is the place for a bachelor supper when ladies are guests. A private room is not proper, and your guests want to see and be seen. The chaperon is seated at the right hand of the host, unless the party is given in honor of a particular woman, in which case she has that place. The chaperon is then at your left. Wraps and coats are taken off in the hall of the restaurant and checked. There is no order of entry, except that the host should precede and the others follow.

MENU EXAMPLES

The usual *menu* for a theater supper is:

I. Clams or oysters on the half shell.
II. Bouillon in cups.
III. Chicken *croquettes* or sweetbreads with peas, or lobster *à la Newburg*.
IV. Terrapin or birds with salad.
V. Ices, cakes, *café noir*, *bonbons*.
VI. *Liqueurs*.

With the oysters or clams white wine is served. Champagne follows the bouillon until the end of the supper.

Dinners at restaurants are frequently given by bachelors, and are followed by a visit to the theater. The rendezvous is either at the house of the chaperon or at the restaurant itself, should the party be limited in number.

The *menu* varies according to the season. Six courses, including raw oysters or clams, soup, fish, *entrée*, roast and vegetables, birds and salad, ices and dessert, are sufficient.

To a man who frequently entertains, and at a particular restaurant, an occasional tip to the head waiter would be of service. This is a word to the wise.

THE HOST'S DUTIES POST-MEAL

After supper the party usually returns to the residence of the chaperon, where the unmarried women have their maids and family escorts awaiting them. The host accompanies them to the chaperon's house, but the other men take leave at the restaurant. The chaperon may have it arranged to have dancing at her house, in which case the party return with her after supper.

A supper in the ladies' annex in nowise differs from this, except that you do not tip the waiter or pay the bill, but have it charged in your monthly account.

Theater clubs are associations of women and men, all subscribing, meeting at the houses of different members, one of whom gives the supper.

Bachelors' dances or *balls* are given at a large hall by a number of unmarried men, who subscribe a certain amount each. A number of well-known matrons are asked to receive the guests, and a cotillion usually follows the supper.

Impromptu lunches, *dinners*, or *suppers* at restaurants sometimes require the immediate settlement of the account. Be careful to draw from your pocketbook a bill of large denomination, and not a handful of change. Do not con over or dispute the items. If you have an account, simply sign the check. If not, it is best to give the waiter his tip and go to the desk and pay while the members of your party are getting their wraps.

STRICTLY FOR MEN

Card parties for the playing of whist, domino, or poker are often given by bachelors at their apartments or residences. In apartments this class of entertainment is only for men. Women should not go to bachelors' apartments except for luncheon, dinner, or supper. In a bachelor's house, however, any entertainment can be given. Small stakes are played for and the usual supper follows. The *farewell bachelor dinner* will have its proper place in the chapter on Wedding Etiquette.

Chapter X

THE COUNTRY HOUSE

BEING A HOSPITABLE BACHELOR

Bachelors, whose incomes are of all sizes and conditions, can have some kind of a country house. It may be a fishing lodge, a hunting box, maintained by three or four men clubbing together; a small cottage plainly and simply furnished at the seashore, near golf links, or in a good neighborhood; or again a large establishment, a villa at Newport or in a fashionable colony with a retinue of servants and a stable filled with horses. Whichever it might be, open hospitality, as much as it is in your power, should prevail. However, never attempt anything more than you can accomplish, and by all means do not run into debt.

HOSTING AT A FISHING OR HUNTING LODGE

To a fishing or hunting lodge men only should be invited. It should be furnished with the mere necessaries, and hung with fishing and hunting prints and trophies of the chase. The hall serves as sitting and even mess room. A man of all work or an old married couple are the best servants. Ample supplies are sent from town, but the leading idea is roughing it, and the table is partially supplied by the game and fish brought back by you and your friends. When the term of the visit of your guests expires, each should be able to bring home a basket of fish or some game. From time to time send to any of your hostesses of the winter something from your preserves. These attentions are much appreciated.

ENTERTAINING AT SMALL COUNTRY VENUES

A truck farm or a small country place near town, which may have either fallen to you by inheritance or which you may have purchased, or which you have for kennels or for your horses, can also be used for entertaining. Even in the largest of these houses the plan of furnishing is substantially the same. There should be a masculine note throughout the entire scheme. The furniture should be old-fashioned, and the pictures sporting and hunting prints and steel engravings. There should be an air of homeliness and open hospitality about the place. It should look as if it were verily Liberty Hall.

GOING THE EXTRA MILE

A tract of unprofitable land could be converted into golf links and a tennis court laid out. A picnic is the popular form in which bachelors who have such a possession may entertain. Some fifty to one hundred people can be invited, and a special train or boat, if the place is too far from the city for a drive, chartered for their accommodation. The invitations should state the hour at which this train or boat would leave the city. Stages await the guests at the country station and bring them up to the house. Cocktails, drinkables, claret cup, tea, and sandwiches are served on their arrival. There should be no fixed programme of amusement. Luncheon, or luncheon and dinner both, according to the length of stay, could be served, and the *menu* should embrace a few courses of country fare. Dancing in the barn during the afternoon will be another form of entertainment, or if you wish to give an elaborate entertainment, vaudeville performers might be hired for the hour after luncheon.

In a large establishment the bachelor who entertains usually has residing with him a sister or female relative who acts as hostess. One of the delights of a wealthy bachelor is to have a large and well-appointed stable with a number of traps which are at the disposition of his guests.

MEETING AND GREETING YOUR GUESTS

A bachelor host always drives to the station or boat to meet his guests. A drag, three-seated surrey, or a station van would be the smart vehicle. I am now writing of a man of large means.

THE ITINERARY

The method of entertaining should be the English one, without any fixed programme for the days of the guests' stay. Only when there is shooting, the party is expected to assemble in the morning. If there is a local club, your men guests should be put up at it, and the entire party made visiting members of the neighboring casino. The rest is conveyed in the advice to have always plenty of good cheer and to entertain the visitors as much as possible. In these houses there is much drinking, possibly, and perhaps cards, but a young man who is a guest should be firm enough to resist temptation, and to stand by his convictions.

PREPARING YOUR GUESTS' ROOMS

One word more, and this applies to many country houses, if not all of them. See that your guests' bedrooms are provided with soap, hair and clothes' brushes, and toilet articles. The desk should be filled with letter paper and envelopes, and if you want to appear very fashionable, the stationery should have the name of your place in blue or red letters at the top or in the right-hand corner of the first sheet. Many convivial souls place on a side table in each room mineral water, cigarettes, cigars, and the inevitable decanter.

YOUR ROLE AS GUEST

When you are a guest you are met at the station by one of your host's traps. Do not be surprised, however, if you do not find this accommodation. It is considered very English, I know not why, to allow bachelors to reach a country house by the best means they can find at the station or landing. You are received by your host, and after refreshment are shown to your room. If you arrive late in the afternoon you do not see your hostess, but dress for dinner and find her in the drawing room when you go downstairs. You are expected to conform to the rules of the house as to the hours for meals, and to place yourself at the service of your hostess. You must certainly appear at any function which has been arranged for you, and it is very impolite to accept, during your stay, any outside invitation to any affair to which your host and hostess have not also been asked. If you have a valet you may bring him with you, but you must certainly notify your host of this intention. Few houses in this country have the accommodations necessary for outside servants.

Tipping is demoralizing, but it is an accepted custom. On your departure after a short stay, at a very fashionable resort, the servant who attends you should have five dollars, the butler five dollars, the coachman five dollars, and the chambermaid two dollars. At smaller places five dollars altogether, judiciously distributed, is ample, or a dollar each to three of the servants.

The first-mentioned amounts can be placed in envelopes and given to the servant attending you for the others. All this is a question of resources, and there are many men who avoid invitations to the large country houses in the East and North because they can not afford the tips. In England, when one is invited to the shooting, one tips the gamekeeper one to five pounds, according to the extent of the bag and duration of visit.

WHAT TO PACK

The usual method of inviting men in this country for a short stay is from Friday or Saturday until Monday. It has often been a puzzle to them as to what they should take in their bag or how much luggage they  should carry. At most not more than a good-sized bag or valise and perhaps a hatbox. For an evening's stay a dress-suit case is sufficient. In your valise must be placed your evening clothes, and if the party is to be somewhat of an informal one, I would also take my dinner jacket. If you are going to a very fashionable resort, a black frock coat, waistcoat, and fancy trousers would not be amiss, but in that case you would have also to take a hatbox for your top hat. Of recent years men in the country have been consulting their comfort more than absolute accuracy in the details of dress. Even at garden parties, at church, and at afternoon teas during the month of August, you seldom see a frock coat or a top hat. Unless you are sure that there will be an occasion where these would be positively required, I would not take them, especially on so short a visit. The linen to be brought should consist of a dress shirt for each evening and a colored shirt for each morning, half a dozen handkerchiefs, two complete changes of underclothes, three pairs of ordinary and two pairs of black silk hose, and a pair of pyjamas. Take three of your ties for day wear and four white lawn for evening, and one black in case you are to use your dinner jacket. Slippers for the bedroom and pumps for evening wear should complete the clothing carried, unless you take your frock coat, when you would have to bring patent leather boots to wear with afternoon dress. I have given rather a liberal allowance of articles for a short stay, but one must be prepared for accidents or emergencies. It is better to take an extra shirt, or a change of underclothes, or a few more ties than one could ordinarily use, so that some *contretemps* would not cause great annoyance and inconvenience. In the absence of a dressing case, care must be taken of the articles for the toilet. The tooth, nail, and shaving brushes, the sponges and washrags, should be packed in little waterproof silk bags, which can be obtained at a small price at any chemist's. Your host or hostess should provide you with soap, but I would not take the risk. I should bring my own in a little metal soapbox or well wrapped in thick paper. Your shaving articles, a shoehorn, button hook, nail file, small pair of nail scissors, tooth powder, or listerine should not be forgotten. The large articles, your combs and your brushes, can all be wrapped separately in tissue paper. It would be gallant of you to bring a box of sweets for your hostess.

If you are asked to play golf, it might be more convenient to travel in your golf togs, which would serve as a lounge suit. But in that case a pair of long trousers to match your coat and waistcoat, or an entire lounge suit should be carried, as on Sunday you would be very uncomfortable in golf dress, and somewhat out of place. Or you might put your "knickers" in the bag, and wear the coat and waistcoat with long trousers.

Chapter XI

A BACHELOR'S SERVANTS

A SERVANT'S DUTIES

As soon as a bachelor begins to branch out a little and to have an apartment or a house or a country establishment, though the latter be only a fishing or a hunting box, he must hire servants. The general servant is perhaps the one most universally employed. Many bachelors hire some middle-aged woman who not only does the cooking, but takes care of the apartment, valets him, and waits at table when he has guests to dinner. Others employ a man to look after them, who is valet and general *factotum*, and others again, with larger establishments, a man and wife. The former does the valeting, the waiting, and is steward and butler, while the woman attends to the cooking and laundry. There are quite a number of bachelor households of this description in our large cities, the occupants being several in number and clubbing together. One is appointed treasurer, and the butler and cook are hired at a stated price and receive a certain sum for catering. When good servants of this kind are found they are treasures.

THE APPEARANCE OF YOUR MANSERVANT

All menservants should be clean shaven. A short bit of side whiskers—*à la* mutton chop—is allowed; but under no circumstances should they have bearded faces or wear a mustache. Their linen and attire should be faultless.

THE MANAGEMENT OF SERVANTS

In the treatment of servants a man must exercise an iron will. He can be kind and considerate, but he must never descend to dispute with one, and certainly not swear at him. To be on familiar terms with one's servants shows the cloven foot of vulgarity. Discharge a servant at once when he is disrespectful or when he is careless in his duties or in his conduct. When asking for anything there is no necessity of forgetting the elements of true politeness, nor is it a blot on your deportment to utter a civil "thank you" for a service performed. All servants should address you as "Sir," and when called should reply "Yes, sir," and certainly not "All right." Your menservants touch their hats to you on receiving orders in the open, on being addressed, and upon your appearance. Encourage your servants now and then by a kind word, and see that they have good and wholesome food, clean and comfortable quarters. Once in a while give them a holiday, or an evening off, a cash remembrance at Christmas, and from time to time some part of your wardrobe or cast-off clothing. In all their movements they should be noiseless and as automatic as possible in their actions.

SPECIFIC TYPES OF SERVANT

And now for particular servants hired by a bachelor:

The *groom* is, with the exception of the general servant, the first domestic likely to be in the employ of an unmarried man of moderate means. When a bachelor becomes a horse owner he can never be too particular about his turnouts and his liveries. The groom in the city or at a fashionable watering place should have two liveries—one for dress occasions and the other for what is known as a "stable suit." The latter, which is a simple English tweed or whipcord, made with a cutaway coat of the same material, will answer perfectly well for the country, where it is ridiculous to have elaborate liveries. A square brown Derby is worn with this suit, brown English driving gloves, and a white plastron or coachman's scarf. This flat scarf is the badge of distinction between the house and stable servant. No tie pin nor trinkets of any description should be allowed servants. The best dress livery is a frock coat, single-breasted, of kersey, the color of your livery; white buckskin riding breeches, top boots, top hat, white plastron, standing collar, and brown driving gloves. One distinctive color should be used, not only for your liveries but also for your traps, as well as one kind of harness. The cockade on the hat is the privilege abroad of ambassadors; it is bad form. Besides the care of your horse or horses, your groom must be a species of outside general servant, ready to go on errands or attend to the numerous duties of a manservant about a country place. By no means can he be substituted for a valet, a butler, or an indoor servant. When he brings your trap to the door he holds the animals' heads until you are seated, when he touches his hat and lets go the reins. If he is to sit behind in the trap he must hold himself upright with folded arms. He alights immediately the trap is stopped, running all errands, and holding the horses until the drive is resumed. He sometimes accompanies his master when the latter rides. He brings his horse to the door and holds it until the mount. He follows, occasionally, on another horse at a respectful distance. Should you be wealthy enough to have also a coachman, your groom can act as second man on the box. A coachman's dress livery consists of a double-breasted long coachman's coat, top boots, and buckskin breeches, white flat plastron, high collar and top hat, and brown driving gloves. When both servants are employed the groom is under the orders of the coachman as regards the stable work.

The Valet.—Of course a valet is a luxury. A man can valet himself very easily, and if the instructions given in the chapters on the Care of Clothes and The Toilet are followed carefully, I hardly think that you would need such a personage. A woman can be perfectly trained to valet a man. Your general servant can also, and is required to fill this position. If you live at a club the club valet will attend to your clothes, and perform the duties of a private servant. There are "valeting companies" organized in many large cities, which take entire charge of your wardrobe, and again there are valets who are hired by several men clubbing together, and who are very capable servants. The individual valet, however, is a very valuable aid to a young bachelor of wealth, especially if he is a man of leisure, or if he goes out a great deal in society. A valet's duties are first and principally the entire charge of his master's wardrobe and toilet, the details of which have been given in previous chapters. They begin an hour or so before the master rises, when clothes are to be pressed and put in order, boots and shoes to be polished and placed on their trees, and the costume of the day to be made ready. If possible, a small room is provided for him as his workshop.

At the hour for rising, the valet enters his master's room very quietly, and, if he is awake, pulls up the shades and lets in the daylight. The bath is then prepared, and while that is being taken the newspapers, mail, and breakfast tray are brought in, and the valet waits for orders. Some men require their valets to shave them, but the majority simply intrust the care of their razors to them, preferring to perform that operation themselves. The valet assists his master in dressing, and, when the toilet is finished, ties or buttons the boots, arranges the spats, and gives a final brush to the clothes. He then fetches the stick, gloves, and hat. During the day he may be employed on errands, in answering tradespeople, in paying bills, or in any minor occupations of that kind. A first-class servant of this character should not only be steward but secretary. When writing letters for his master he should write them in the third person, and also sign them "Respectfully yours, John Smith, *valet*."

A valet is told of the engagements of the day, and has the clothes arranged accordingly, and he must be at his post. In the evening the dress suit is laid out, with choice of ties and two coats, the formal and informal, or Tuxedo. A valet must be at the rooms when his master retires. In traveling he takes care of the luggage, tickets, and all the little annoying details. He travels second class abroad, and in this country he should never be allowed to be a passenger in a drawing-room car with his master. The valet wears no livery. He dresses quietly in a plain sack suit of dark material, and wears a Derby hat. Should he be required to wait on table, he dresses in semi-livery if the affair is a luncheon, and in evening dress if it is a dinner.

The *butler* is a very rare functionary in a bachelor's establishment, only the wealthiest being able to afford him. The valet or general servant acts as butler, and when in this position he should always have a black coat on when answering the bell.

I have used the terms throughout this chapter of "master" and "servant." Employer and employee are correct only when the relations between the two persons are not of a domestic character.

Chapter XII

THE DANCE

CHARITY BALLS

Of absolutely public balls the only one which society attends is the Charity. Tickets to the Charity are sold by a number of lady patronesses, and you are apt to receive one or several from some of them, if you are a rich young man, with a request to purchase. If the note states that you are expected to be a guest you are simply to answer it, as you would any other invitation, and certainly not to inclose any money. Patronesses frequently are named because it is expected that they will purchase quite a number of tickets. And here let me give a useful hint. In sending money to this and for charitable entertainments in general, always do it by check; never inclose bills. If you must use cash, keep it for your small tradespeople.

Everything may be said to have its price at a Charity Ball. Supper is sometimes included with the ticket. The repast is usually rather poor, but then you must remember it is for charity.

PARTICIPATING IN THE GRAND MARCH

Perhaps you will be asked some time in advance by the patronesses to be one in the "grand march." The "grand march" proper is a form of exhibition long since relegated to balls of the "Tough Boys' Coterie" and other assemblages of the same class. But it has survived, in place of a lancers or quadrille of honor, at the Charity Ball, and we have either to go through with it or watch it from the boxes with Christian patience. If you are to take part, I would advise you to present yourself at the hall or opera house about nine o'clock. The floor manager will do the rest. You are to offer your left arm to the lady you are taking out, and you march around the place in regular line, sometimes once, sometimes twice, and the agony is over. The company assembled does not join in this ceremony, and the formation of figures and countermarches is an affair in vogue at balls of a different class, which I should imagine none of my readers would patronize or even "hear tell of," except through the newspapers.

BEING ASKED TO THE BALL

Your first intimation may be while visiting at the house of one of the patrons or patronesses, when your hostess or host may ask you if you would like to go to the Assembly or the Patriarchs'. If you have no other engagement for that evening—and I think it would be policy for you to make others subservient to this—you should reply that you would be delighted to do so. Your host or hostess will then say that he or she will send you a ticket. This may be one way, or you may receive a note asking if you are free for that particular date, whether "would you like to go to the Assembly?" etc., or again, you might simply receive a note with a ticket. In any one of these cases, just as soon as you receive the ticket you must answer your correspondent immediately, accepting, or, if you can not go, regretting and returning it. You must remember that all tickets are personal and each Patriarch or each patroness has only a certain number.

I would, if there were time between the date for the ball and the reception of your ticket, call or leave cards personally on your hostess or host for the evening, according to rules in a former chapter.

ENTERING THE BALLROOM

The evening arrives. Balls and dances are theoretically supposed to begin at ten o'clock. You can safely go a little after eleven. You will be early enough. Your ticket is received, your hat and coat removed, your hat check given, and you proceed to the ballroom.

It is almost needless for me to tell you how to dress for this occasion. At dances of any kind, formal evening dress is required.

On entering the room, if it is at the Assembly, you will encounter a line of patronesses. You should make a low, sweeping bow to them and, if convenient, speak to your hostess, be it only a few words of greeting. If not at that time, select a later hour in the evening. No one shakes hands.

You look around to find your friends and acquaintances. At the Patriarchs' the chaperons sit upon a raised platform, or dais, I might call it, all together. Their charges, once away from them, are around the rooms.

THE DREADED DANCING CARD

In nearly all the cities, except New York, every guest is provided with a dancing card, which makes the keeping of dancing engagements a part of the festivity. New

York is too large for such things, and dancing cards have been relegated to the realms of innocuous desuetude. However, if you are at a ball or a dance in another city where they are used, your first duty would be to have your engagements filled. You should remain with your partner after each dance until her next cavalier appears.

New Yorkers are sensible, if only for this reason, for having banished the dance card. It is hard for a man to tell a woman he must leave her, but I think it is better by far to do so than to appear rude to your succeeding partner. A woman who has so little regard for you and such selfish consideration for herself does not deserve to be handled with gloves. And yet it needs a heroic soul to abandon her in a crowded ballroom, even if it is to lead her back to her chaperon.

ASKING FOR A DANCE

You exchange greetings with the women you know, and if you wish to ask one of them to dance, you say, "May I have the pleasure of this turn with you?" or "Can I have a turn with you?" It is absolutely impossible to keep dance engagements, and you are obliged, perhaps, to snatch a dance whenever you can get it. After your turn you must always manage to stop at about the point where you began. You will be sure to find your partner's chaperon just at that place. There are two reasons for this—one is that the man with whom your partner has engaged weeks, if not months, before to dance the cotillion has reserved his chairs there, and she has told many of her friends just about in which part of the ballroom she may be found; and another is that women, under all circumstances, keep a distinctive place in a ballroom.

A gentleman never dances without gloves. He always puts them on before entering the ballroom. A man should dance easily and gracefully, and look as if he were enjoying himself. He should be careful about guiding and not running into people. Swinging the hands is vulgar and unsightly. The waltz seems to survive all other forms of dancing, but there is every now and then a revival of the polka. Two steps and fancy dances are the vogue at summer hotels, but not at smart functions.

DANCES OF THE DAY

The quadrille of to-day is the simple lancers, and some years ago it was a silly fad to pretend not to remember the figures. A little life and spirit are sometimes introduced in the lancers when the gathering is small, and among intimate friends there is more or less occasion for it. The barn dance has gone out of fashion entirely in America, but our English cousins, especially those living in the country and in Suburbia, are very fond of it. Balls frequently end with Sir Roger de Coverley, the English form of the Virginia reel.

FOOD IS SERVED

About two o'clock supper is announced, and this is done all over the world, I believe, by the strains of the Priests' March in Norma. You should settle this with your

partner, and as supper is served at tables of parties of four
or six, an agreeable quartette or sextette can be secured.
Parties are never less than four, and a girl who sups
alone with a man, even at the Patriarchs', is considered
very fast, and by such impudent behavior would lose
caste. You should arrange with your partner, therefore,
to be as near the supper-room door as possible about
the supper hour. There is always a rush and a crush, and
no tables are reserved except those for the patronesses
or the Patriarchs. Two of the party should get in early
and reserve the table and wait until the rest arrive. Ball
suppers are nearly all alike. Four or five courses, which
commence with oysters, are followed by bouillon, and
then terrapin and birds, and salad and ices, fruit and coffee.
Three kinds of wine are served, and champagne forms the
chief. Many matrons even will not allow their daughters
to go to supper without being chaperoned, and so when
you ask your partner she will sometimes have her parents
obtain the table. Should you be asked to the table of one
of the patronesses, you will have a partner provided for
you. Remember the first engagement should always be
kept, and if a patroness should honor you with such an
invitation, and you have made prior arrangements, you
should at once explain by note your position, which will
be a sufficient excuse to your would-be hostess.

After supper the cotillion, or German, as it is sometimes
called, is danced.

Chapter XIII

THE COTILLION

A BRIEF HISTORY

At large balls, there is hardly time for more than two or three figures and one favor figure. It is almost useless for me to go into the history of the cotillion, and I do not believe that it would be of any service to my readers. We imported it from France about the same time as the English, and it owes its origin, I believe, to Germany. For the past thirty years it has been a favorite form of dance. It is picturesque and amusing, and, besides, gives the opportunity for the exchange among the dancers of pretty trifles provided by the generosity of the host. At large semipublic balls like the Patriarchs' (I use "semipublic" simply because given by a number and not in a private house) the favors are very simple, but at special cotillions or at those danced at private houses they are extremely elaborate and costly.

CLAIMING YOUR SEAT

Cotillion seats are generally secured in the early part of the evening by tying handkerchiefs to the backs of the chairs. At the Patriarchs' and other large balls they can be secured by arrangement with one of the stewards, as each Patriarch has so many reserved for him, and the man invited by one of them can obtain permission and ask for two of his host's seats. But this is not usual, and is known as a "little trick of the trade."

REQUIREMENTS OF LEADING THE DANCE

To be a successful leader of cotillions it requires the skill and the tact of a general—I might almost say of a Napoleon Bonaparte. One's talents should not be altogether in one's heels and one's toes. The leader must be an excellent dancer and a firm disciplinarian. He must see that the wall flowers have an occasional turn, and that every one gets at least one favor. As he has to marshal a large force of people he is bound to find among them—of course in the orthodox society manner—a few turbulent spirits, a few who would mutiny, and who must be taught their places in a conciliatory but positive manner.

The cotillion is generally danced after supper. It lasts about two hours. At large balls two figures are all that can be danced, owing to the number of guests. Sometimes it is led by two couples. A leader frequently dances stag—that is, without a partner. All men dancing without partners are called stags. These usually have their place by the door and are given their turn last. The leader must announce after supper the time for the cotillion to begin. He must see that the partners are all in their places. The favor table is generally placed at the end of the room opposite the doors, but this depends on the shape and the style of the apartment.

Formerly a cotillion leader used a whistle for the different figures; to-day, however, he simply claps his hands to denote the changes.

THE LOGISTICS OF THE DANCE

It is almost unnecessary here to illustrate the form of the cotillion. It consists in waltzes and sometimes polkas, danced by eight, ten, or twelve couples at a time. The couples are seated in chairs around the room, the men without partners known as the stags being near the door. The leader begins the first figure, which is usually the simplest one, by "taking out" or choosing a partner and motioning the first four, six, or eight couples with places nearest him on one or both sides of the room to rise. All waltz. After a turn around the room the leader stops and claps his hands. The partners all separate, and each of them goes and chooses a new one—the man a new woman, the woman who was his partner a new man. The figure is then arranged and danced. After the evolution required by the figure is finished there is another short waltz, and the dancers return to their places. The leader then calls out the next party, and this is repeated until every one in the room has had a turn. The stags are called out last. Having no partners to dance with, each has the privilege of taking out two ladies—the first before the figure is formed, and the second when the change of partners is signalled by the leader. The leader directs the figures and dances all the time.

THE DISTRIBUTION OF THE FAVORS

Every second figure is one for the distribution of favors. The same procedure occurs, and when the leader claps his hands the dancers separate, waiting for the favors to be distributed. The latest custom is for the leader and his partner to carry around the favors, to the couples whose turn comes next. He gives to the ladies, she to the men. The scramble at the favor table has been abolished. The men present their favors to the new partners whom they select, and the women do likewise. It is very embarrassing and not good form to give your favor to the partner with whom you are dancing the cotillion. Favors must be sufficient in quantity not only to go once all around, but there should be some left over, as the advent of the stags gives the ladies a double chance to bestow favors upon men. The most graceful way of offering a favor is to present it with a little bow. Try and locate the places where your friends are sitting. It is certainly rude, if not tantalizing, to search through a long row of girls dangling a favor. It is not difficult in the figures to become well acquainted with the local geography. Matrons are asked frequently to preside at the favor tables, but recently some of the floral trifles are brought in arranged in a sedan chair of flowers, at which two powdered lackeys are stationed, like the linkboys of old. Originality, however, has not been rampant in cotillions. Favor figures are the most popular. The woman who brings the greatest number of favors from a cotillion scores an undoubted triumph. She comes from the ballroom flushed and delighted, carrying with her the trophies of her victory, which she is pleased to call her "scalps." Social obligations are often paid off by men in this way.

DIFFERENT TYPES OF COTILLIONS

Of the few cotillion figures danced, the *grand chain* is the most popular and the simplest. The number of couples called by the leader form themselves in a ring around the room. At his signal they face each other and dance the right and left grand chain, the men to the right and the women to the left, until the original parties are brought together, when all waltz.

The *Sir Roger de Coverley figure* is formed in lines of four abreast, the men standing together on the inside, and the women next to their partners on the outside of the line. When the leader signals, the women advance quickly, one after the other, to the head of the line. The men then join hands, forming an arch, as in Sir Roger de Coverley; the women, passing under two by two, meeting their partners, waltz with them.

In the *snake figure*—one which is very seldom danced— quite a large number of couples are called, who form a ring around the room. The leader, taking the hand of one of the men, breaks the chain, and the couples are wound around until they come together in a knot, when the signal is given to them to waltz. The *wheel figure* is somewhat similar, and is quite a romp.

In the *ring figure* another evolution is borrowed from the lancers. Rings of four couples form through the room. The men raise their arms and the women pass through, dancing with the men in the next ring, and so on, until they get to the top of the room, the men remaining stationary. Then a grand march, men to the left, ladies to the right, is formed, and the partners meet and dance.

The *Maypole* and all complicated figures which require the use of toys or *papier-maché* articles are not in vogue. In Paris these trifles, such as vegetables and heads of animals and other gewgaws, pass for favors, as well as to lend a variety to the cotillion. In New York very handsome souvenirs have superseded these.

Frequently in large cotillions in the blank or nonfavor figures are danced only once without change of partners, as in the snake or grand chain; otherwise the cotillion would be interminable. The leader calls out a number of couples and goes through the figure at once, the original partners dancing all the time with each other. I have given both forms, and although the first explanation may seem to those who go out every year antiquated, it is still the vogue for small and consequently enjoyable cotillions.

Chapter XIV

A BACHELOR'S LETTERS

THE BEAUTY OF LETTERS

Letter writing is an art, and there is no pleasure equal to that of receiving and reading a chatty and well-worded epistle from some dear friend. I have some packets of letters preserved to-day that I read and reread. They are always fresh and interesting to me. They are a complete index to the character of the writer, and they serve, after long years have passed, to bring up again delightful pictures of days and scenes which were brighter.

THE DANGERS OF LETTERS

However, there is one rule a man must observe: never keep a compromising letter—if you should receive one—especially from a woman. Sometimes women are foolish and careless, and they allow their pens to run away with them. They bitterly regret their folly, and the very idea that there exists somewhere a packet of letters which would bring serious trouble, if not ruin, upon them and those they love, is a cause of constant grief and worry. I know that there are letters written by one once dear, but now perhaps turned fickle or false, or separated from us forever, from which we feel loath to part; but we must be men and reduce to ashes what would hurt in the very least degree or cast a reflection upon an innocent if silly woman. Suppose you were to die suddenly, and among your papers these letters were found, with you alone, dumb in death, perhaps, only able to vindicate the unfortunate writer. We must think of those things. They belong to the *personnel* not only of a true gentleman, but they appeal to our common sense.

A TIP FROM THE AUTHOR

Character is frequently judged by handwriting. Write a good, clear, legible hand, without any flourishes, and always use the best and the blackest of ink.

THE BASICS OF LETTER-WRITING

The typewriter is employed only for business correspondence.

For social correspondence use only Irish-linen white note paper, unruled, with square envelopes to match. Fancy or tinted note paper of any kind is vulgar. If you have a permanent residence your address can be legibly engraved in one color, usually blue or scarlet, at the head of the first sheet. If you are a member of a club, the club note paper is proper for all social correspondence. If you want to, use your crest in lieu of address, but this practice is somewhat strained in this country. Always add the date in writing. In letters, the day, the month, and the year should be written. In notes you only put the day—for instance, "Saturday the twenty-second." The best signature is "Sincerely yours," and not "Yours sincerely." In England the quaint "Faithfully yours" is used for business correspondence. Tradespeople and servants only sign "Respectfully yours."

ADDRESSING PEOPLE IN THE CORRECT MANNER

In America we "esquire" all men who are our equals. A butcher, a baker, a tailor or other person, when we order supplies, we address as "Mr." The abbreviation "Esq." is the usual form. In England you would write to a duke and address the letter "The Duke of Buckingham"; to a knight, "Sir Thomas Appleby"; to an earl or a marquis, "Lord Dufferin"— that is, supposing the letter would be a social one.

In writing to a friend or in answer to an invitation or a note, you would begin, "My dear Mrs. Brown," "My dear Mr. Brown," or even "My dear Brown," but never "Dear Miss Brown," "Dear Mrs. Brown," or "Dear Brown," unless you were on terms of great intimacy with them. But if the letter is a strictly business one, and the term "Sir" or "Sirs" is used, then you would be obliged to drop the possessive pronoun. A very formal or a business letter would begin thus:

John Smith, Esq.,
#22 Pacific Avenue, Brooklyn, N. Y.
Dear Sir:

and not "My dear Sir."

A business letter to a woman demands, however, the possessive "My," thus: "My dear Madam."

To a firm, one writes:

Messrs. John Smith & Co.,
Dear Sirs:

and never "Gentlemen"—a most ridiculous form of address.

The clergy are addressed "Reverend and dear Sir." A bishop is "Right Reverend and dear Sir," and an archbishop "Most Reverend and dear Sir." In this republican country all other dignitaries can be addressed as "Dear Sir."

SIGNED, SEALED, DELIVERED

Formal invitations are written in the third person, also letters addressed to tradespeople.

The address on a letter should be written about the middle of the envelope, the street and number a little to the right, and the name of the city and State in the corner.

The stamp should be placed neatly in the right-hand corner. The mail to-day is almost the quickest means of delivery, and a special ten-cent stamp will insure, in a large city, a more prompt reception of your epistle than if you intrusted it to the tender mercies of a messenger boy.

Your paper should fold once in the middle. There is nothing so awkward or so apt to give a bad impression as a letter improperly folded. It is bulky and unsightly. Private letters should always be sealed with wax, in color dark green or red. Black is used for mourning. In sealing a letter be careful to make a neat effect, and not to smear the wax all over the envelope. The seal is then stamped with your monogram, or, if you insist upon it, with your crest, but never with your coat of arms. For the purpose of sealing letters men use their seal rings or a little stamp which can be obtained at any silversmith's. When writing from the club you can use the club stamp. Business letters are moistened and gummed, a little damp sponge being used for this purpose. To moisten envelopes with the tongue is nasty.

Letters written on hotel or business paper should be confined to the commercial world. Your friends and acquaintances should not receive them. Sometimes, when writing from a very interesting place to a very intimate friend or to relatives, hotel paper may be used, as you would like your correspondent to see a picture of the house at which you are stopping.

Every gentleman should, however, carry in his portmanteau a flat portfolio with writing materials and a traveling inkstand.

DIFFERENT TYPES OF LETTERS

Your personal correspondence should be a reflection of yourself. Be pithy, bright, and witty. Give the news and innocent gossip, but beware of making statements in letters which you can not substantiate. Above all, think twice before you pen a harsh or an unkind word, even if a reproof be merited.

In business letters be brief and to the point.

There are two kinds of letters which sometimes puzzle the writer—letters of condolence and letters of congratulation. A letter of condolence—as will be explained in the chapter on Funerals—is due from you at the death of a near or dear friend to the relative or relatives—if you feel that you know them all well enough to address more than one epistle of sympathy— nearest and dearest to the deceased. Usually one letter is sufficient, but sometimes it may occur that you feel that you should also write to others. Make it as natural as possible. Avoid all stilted phrases and studied efforts at consolation. A few words is all that is necessary. If you have been on intimate terms with the family wire them your sympathy, and write a week or so afterward.

Letters of congratulation are much easier to compose. On the occasion of the announcement of an engagement of a friend, or in answer to his letter announcing the happy event, or on the arrival of any good fortune to those of whom you are fond or for whom you have a high regard, a letter of congratulation is necessary or acceptable. All letters announcing sad or joyous news should receive an immediate reply.

Chapter XV

THE BACHELOR'S CLUB

THE IN THING

Club life is a growth of recent years. It is now so firmly established, and it is so popular that there is not a village or even a settlement which has not at least its casino, or its little coterie organized for golf, tennis, athletic, or merely social enjoyment. All of these, from the great metropolitan clubs of the cities down to the very humblest in the "wilds," are governed by club laws and are regulated by club etiquette.

CLUB EXCLUSIVITY

In New York, now a city of clubs, this etiquette differs much from that observed in London, Paris, or any of the large continental centers. In London, a man is identified with his club. He rarely belongs to more than one, and his membership there denotes his social standing, his pursuits in life, and, above all, his politics. English clubs are also very jealous of admittance of strangers, and are not in the least hospitable to the foreigner. There are exceptions to this among the literary, theatrical, and Bohemian organizations, but the Pall Mall clubs are "closed." In New York, Boston, Chicago, and other American cities there are organizations which insist upon certain qualifications, such as being a university man, a lawyer, an author, a physician, or a member of a college fraternity, for admittance; but then the members also belong to other clubs, where their social standing, or perhaps the extent of their bank account, is their passport.

A PROMOTION IN SOCIETY

If a man wishes to get on socially, he should belong to at least one good club. It gives him his standing in the community, and places him. He is no longer on the list of the unidentified.

HOW TO BECOME A MEMBER

When a choice is made of a club which you desire to join, the next step would be to have two members in good standing to act as your sponsors—one proposes your name and the other seconds. A good sponsor is necessary, and you should choose one who has many friends in the organization of which you desire to become a member. The president, officers, and the governing committee are debarred from either proposing or seconding a name for membership. The term of a man's novitiate depends upon the state of the waiting list. Your proposer will notify you when your name will be reached, as he himself will be notified in writing by the committee on membership. The rules of candidacy differ in various clubs. In some, the name of the candidate with those of the two members proposing him is exposed in a conspicuous place where the entire club can see it. There is also a book in which other members sign the application, and the number of signatures, of course, has weight with the governors.

Again, the name is inscribed in a book kept for the purpose in the steward's office, and it is not necessary that any other indorsement except that of your sponsors be made.

ANY OBJECTIONS?

Any member objecting to the name of a candidate has two methods by which he can make known his objection. One is to write directly to the governors, or to the committee on admissions and membership, whichever, according to the laws of the club, has the matter in hand. Usually it is the governing committee or board of governors. This communication is treated, as are all club matters, with the secrecy of the confessional. Your sponsors are written to and the objections stated, but the name of the person objecting is withheld. The other method is, if any one has an objection to your admission, that he should go at once in a manly way to one of your sponsors and state it. It is a rare occurrence in a New York club that any candidate is black-balled. The warning from the governing committee, or from another member to the sponsors, is a word to the wise, and the men who propose you should immediately withdraw your name to avoid a disaster. Otherwise a very great risk is run, as objections which have any foundation have great weight with the governing committee.

In the clubs where the names of the candidates are kept only in a small book, while on the waiting list they are posted ten days before the election in a conspicuous part of the clubhouse.

REQUIREMENTS OF A CANDIDATE

No candidate can be elected to a club who is not personally known to two or more members of the governing committee. A short time before election, if the candidate has not this acquaintance, it is the duty of his sponsors to take him around and introduce him, or to arrange that he will meet these gentlemen in some way; otherwise his name will go over; and after two setbacks of this kind, it will be rejected.

On the election of a candidate—the balloting being done by the governing committee—the sponsors are notified, sometimes by posting and otherwise simply by letter. The secretary of the club will let the new member know immediately of his election, and the letter, which is usually a form, will also notify him that his admission fee and yearly dues are payable. The admission or entrance fee to a club is from one hundred to two hundred dollars in the well-known New York organizations, and the yearly dues are from seventy-five to one hundred dollars. These must be paid at once by check. The rules of most clubs allow a thirty-day limit. If you are so fortunate as to be admitted after the date of the yearly meeting, you will only be liable for one half the current yearly dues; otherwise you pay the entire amount.

It is now the duty of the sponsors to introduce their newly elected candidate to the club. This is an easy matter. One of them will go with you, sit in the general smoking or lounging room, and make you acquainted with one or two of his friends. The responsibility is then over.

CLUB RULES AND REGULATIONS

Club etiquette is very simple. It is only the application of the usual rules of courtesy observed in private life. The club is your home. You should behave there as you would in your own house as host, and consequently your conduct toward your fellow-members should be characterized by the utmost consideration.

The average clubhouse has a large room on the ground or first floor which is used for smoking, reading, the newspapers, and "living" generally. On the floors above there are the dining rooms, the library, and reading and card rooms. The billiard room occupies a special quarter, according to the plan of the house.

A clever man said that there was but one rule of clubhouse etiquette different from the general laws of manners, and that was to keep your hat on. This is true, but then there are many others. Men do not take off their hats on entering a club, and do not remove them in any room except that in which they dine. All social clubs are more or less "closed." Visitors are only allowed under certain restrictions. The general rule is that a member may invite to the use of the club for a period of ten consecutive days any one not a resident of the city, but can have no more than one guest at a time. No stranger shall be introduced a second time unless he shall have been absent from the city three months. In some clubs a member may introduce as a visitor a resident of the city, but he can have no more than one such guest at a time. No person shall be introduced more than once in twelve months. Other clubs are open to the admission of visitors at certain periods, and others again have ladies' days, at which a reception to the fair friends of the members is given. All this depends on the rules of the club. As soon as you are made a member you are given a little book in which these are contained, and you should study them carefully. The name of a guest should be entered on the visitors' book with that of his host. If the visitor is put up for a certain period a card to the club is sent him, and during his stay he has all the privileges of a member. He can run up an account, but he should certainly settle it before his term expires, otherwise his host will be held responsible.

A clubman never pays an attendant for refreshment or food served. Gratuities of any kind to servants are forbidden. When refreshment is required, you press the electric bell, of which there are a number in all the rooms, and the attendant comes to you for your order. When he brings it he has with it a check which you sign. These checks are, of course, debited to you, and you receive your bill once a month, or you can make arrangements to pay at the steward's or cashier's desk daily.

You order your meals in the same manner, and when they are ready, the servant will notify you.

At most of the clubs smoking is not permitted in the dining rooms until after nine, nor are refreshments allowed to be served in the visitors' room or library at any time. Books and magazines are not to be removed from the reading room or library, nor any publication belonging to the club from the clubhouse.

There is still a prejudice against pipe smoking in many of the clubs, and you must consult the rules before you attempt this practice. A man does not remove his coat or sit in his shirtsleeves in any of the public rooms. An allowance, however, is made in the billiard room.

The loud-voiced man is one of the nuisances of a club. Loud talking may be endured in the smoking or general room, but certainly not in the library or the reading rooms.

The "kicker" is another objectionable person. He should remember that the best way of rectifying abuses is to send to the house committee all complaints of any deficiency in the service of the club, of overcharges, mistakes, or defects. The club is not a place to conduct one's commercial interests. Invitations and special correspondence can be conducted on club paper, but certainly it is a breach of club etiquette to use it for business purposes.

The man who bows to a woman from a club window is not a gentleman. By this action he fastens upon her the most disgraceful odium one of her sex can bear.

The name of a woman should never be whispered in a club unless it is to say something complimentary of her. Even this is not in good taste.

It is not club etiquette to "treat." You can do so if you desire, but you are not obliged to follow this inane custom, which is born of bar-room ethics.

All the affairs of a club must be regarded in strict confidence. Under no consideration should that which has occurred within these sacred portals be divulged to outsiders.

Once a year—usually at Christmas—a subscription is taken up for the employees and servants. From five to ten dollars is the proper amount to give.

A few clubs have a ladies' restaurant attached, where members may take their families or give dinners, or where the wives of members have the privilege of giving luncheons or other entertainments. Otherwise ladies are not admitted to the privileges of the clubhouse, except on ladies' days, and where there is an "annex" they can only avail themselves of that part set aside for their convenience upon the authority of a member.

Chapter XVI

THE SPORTING BACHELOR

A HORSEY HOBBY

Driving.—Driving really comprises coaching as well as the tandem.

A man who has any pretensions whatever to keeping his own horses or driving should be judged by the appearance of his traps. He submits himself to what one, to-day, might call the X-ray of criticism. He enters a field, and he must be weighed in the balance and his position defined by the standard of his associates. In the first place, your horses must be well groomed, their hoofs blackened, and their tails properly banged. I do not intend here to enter a discussion concerning the cruelty of docking horses' tails. The social law is without exception. Horses with long tails are impossible. I believe banging is not accompanied by any physical pain.

The harness, the trap itself, the coachman, and groom or grooms should be as immaculate as the horses. There should not be a single item out of gear. Every detail must be perfect. Choose some individual color for your traps, and never change the colors of your stable any more than you would your liveries. I have discussed fully in the chapter on Servants the duties of coachmen and grooms, and I refer the reader to that section of this book for information concerning liveries and the human *personnel* of your trap.

As to the color of your horses you should consult the fashion of the moment. To-day grays and bays are matched, and a person in half mourning recently appeared on a leading thoroughfare with a black trap and harness and white horses.

A bachelor, however, should court simplicity, and I do not even approve of an equipage with two men on the box for an unmarried man. In fact I do not know of a single bachelor who has such a turnout.

A coach, a tandem, a drag, or any of the array of fashionable carts, or a private hansom should limit the list.

DRIVING DRESS

Coolness and absolute confidence are the requisite virtues of good driving.

The driver salutes always with the whip; those on the coach with him or in the trap bow.

Dress for driving in the city is usually that of afternoon, and a high hat is indispensable. Sometimes the huge gray coats with large buttons and a gray topper are worn. Dogskin driving gloves and driving boots complete the costume. In the country one wears tweed or Scotch cheviot and a Derby hat.

DRIVING WITH DECORUM

The man who drives mounts last, his horses' heads being held by the groom. His whip should be in its socket; the reins loosely thrown over the horses' backs. He should spring into his seat and start immediately.

There is a certain smartness in driving, in the way you manage your whip, your horses, and the many other details, which it is the province of a good master of the sport to teach you.

Remember, however, that the secret of your mastery over your stables should be your perfect knowledge of every detail. If you are a novice you should begin by learning the name and use of each part of your harness. You should be able to tell at a glance if everything is right, and you can not be too severe if anything is out of gear or the animals are not properly groomed. The best position on the box is a firm seat with your feet close together. Drive with one hand and keep the whip hand free, except for its legitimate use in touching your horses now and then, and in saluting.

A man always sits with his back to the horses in a Victoria, or any other four-seated vehicle, when there are two ladies with him. When there is only one he sits by her side. He alights first with a view to assisting the ladies. He gets in last.

It is not good form in New York for unmarried couples to drive together, unaccompanied by a chaperon. It is permitted at Newport and the country and seaside resorts, but a groom always sits on the back seat. In this case the woman is frequently the whip.

A man and a woman may drive together in the city in a hansom, although this is considered unconventional.

HORSE RIDING

Riding, since the advent of the wheel, is not as fashionable an amusement in cities as formerly.

Riding classes, which meet two evenings during the week, are still very popular. These gatherings take place

at a riding academy, and a
competent riding master
is in charge.

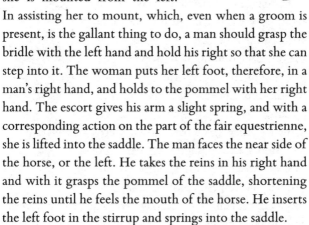

When riding with a
woman, a man should always
be at her right. A woman's
riding habit falls to the left and
she is mounted from the left.
In assisting her to mount, which, even when a groom is
present, is the gallant thing to do, a man should grasp the
bridle with the left hand and hold his right so that she can
step into it. The woman puts her left foot, therefore, in a
man's right hand, and holds to the pommel with her right
hand. The escort gives his arm a slight spring, and with a
corresponding action on the part of the fair equestrienne,
she is lifted into the saddle. The man faces the near side of
the horse, or the left. He takes the reins in his right hand
and with it grasps the pommel of the saddle, shortening
the reins until he feels the mouth of the horse. He inserts
the left foot in the stirrup and springs into the saddle.

In speaking of a pommel, I wish it understood that the
English saddle is used, which has no visible pommel, but
that part of it is still called by the name in lieu of another
term.

A good rider should never mount from a horse block
or a fence. The English mode of riding is fashionable.
The smart pace is a short canter. In trotting, a man may
rise to the trot. Squaring the elbows is a trifle vulgar and
obsolete. In meeting acquaintances, a man should bow. A
man accompanying a lady should always keep pace with

her, and never either go ahead or let his horse fall behind. A man riding alone should never pass or catch up with a woman unattended.

RIDING DRESS

When one rides it is only in the morning. Afternoon riding is not the vogue it was. For years the fashionable afternoon riding costume was a black cutaway or morning coat, ordinary trousers strapped under the ordinary walking boot, top hat, and gloves, but the present riding costume for the morning consists of whipcord or corduroy riding breeches and jacket, brown leather waistcoat, brown Derby hat, boots or leggings, and dark gloves. You can wear this in the afternoon, but the ordinary costume is considered smarter and more convenient. The evening classes always end with a supper and a dance. The woman's habit is easily changed, but to appear at night in riding costume or with boots in a drawing room is certainly absurd. To wear evening dress on horseback, even a Tuxedo coat, is also outlandish, and thus the compromise has been effected, and the old black diagonal cutaway brought into use.

HUNTING DRESS

Riding to hounds requires special knowledge as to the rules and the etiquette of the different hunts. These vary.

The meet is generally at some farm or country house, and you are expected to appear in the regulation hunt colors. The orthodox costume is morning coat, white or fancy waistcoat, riding breeches, top boots, crop, top hat, and hunting scarf. The master of the hounds should wear a red or scarlet frock coat and hunting cap. After the hunt there is a breakfast, and several times during the year a ball. At the latter festivity, members of the club should wear their scarlet evening coats.

A COACH PARTY

Coaching is yet another of the intricate arts. I will give a few points to the novice. The place of honor is the box seat and should be given to a lady, when ladies are of the party.

If a bachelor is a good whip, a coaching party is an excellent way for him to entertain. The start should be from some fashionable locality in town, and eight or ten is a large party. It is needless for me to call the attention of a whip to the importance of his drag and horses and appointments being perfect. During the progress of the coach the guard who sits in the rear blows his horn at regular intervals. A bugle or cornet is not good form, although I have heard it in small towns.

It may seem elementary, but for the requirements of those who have never coached I might as well state that the guests sit on the top and not inside the coach. A neat and serviceable team may be made with two browns as leaders and a brown and a bay as wheelers. To the novice the names of these will indicate their position.

A coaching route should be about ten to fifteen miles. A halt is made at a country club, of which the host is a member, or a hotel, where luncheon is served. The *menu* consists of the usual comestibles with plenty of champagne. Two hours altogether are allowed for rest, and then the start homeward is made. The whip should wear driving costume, with gray or black high hat. The men guests can be dressed in morning costume, tweeds, and Derby hats, unless the occasion is one of formality, such as a coaching parade, when one should don afternoon dress. The general etiquette of driving applies to coaching.

A WHEEL REVOLUTION

Wheeling is the popular and fashionable amusement at present writing, and it bids fair to continue so until quite late in the twentieth century. As yet there are no special rules of etiquette for this new sport, except that which would govern its dress. Otherwise there are the rules of the road—keeping and turning to the right—and the extending by gentlemen of those civilities which they should never forget to the fair sex, and consideration for their fellow-men. A man should always wait for a lady to mount, holding the bicycle. He should ride at her left, keeping pace with her, and sufficiently near to be of assistance in case of an accident. He should dismount first and help her to do so if necessary. The present fashionable costume for cycling consists of tweed knickers and short lounge jacket of same material, brown leather or linen waistcoat, colored shirt, with white turn-down collar and club tie, golf stockings, and low-quartered tan wheeling shoes. A cap of tweed to match the suit completes the rig. At cycling clubs black small clothes with dinner jacket may be worn, but as yet it is not the prevailing fashion.

In summer very natty wheeling costumes are made of linen or crash.

One word more as to wheeling. Owing to its popularity, many have sought to make it vulgar and common. An idea that a man has the privilege of addressing any woman on a bicycle is most erroneous. You would not offer such an impertinence to an equestrienne, and you must remember that a "wheel" is only a metal horse.

GAME FOR GAME

Shooting deserves a few words, although shooting parties in the acceptance of the foreign and British entertainments have as yet but few counterparts in this country. Men chase the aniseed bag or an imported fox when riding to hounds, and when they take gun in hand it is for the purpose of hunting big game. In England you may be invited for the shooting. The start is in the morning, in a party accompanied by the gamekeepers. The birds are flurried, the guns are loaded by your special attendant, and you only pause in your work of destruction for luncheon, which is served somewhere in the woods or on the moors. You are expected to be at the house about four, where, after changing your clothes, you appear in the drawing room for tea. You are cautioned in these parties, in order to avoid accident, before crossing a hedge, gate, or any other obstacle, to remove your cartridges. You are to be unusually careful in the manner of holding your gun, and should certainly not flourish it around or point it at any living thing, save that which it is intended to kill. Guns used as walking sticks or props to take flying leaps or other extraordinary purposes are the assinine diversions of some idiots. In England a position is assigned to you. It is etiquette to remain in it, shooting in a liberal and sportsmanlike spirit, accepting shots as they come. The gamekeepers expect a tip at the end of the visit. The correct dress is loose jacket, knicker corduroy breeches, stout ribbed stockings, and box-cloth leggings. Heavy russet boots and a cloth shooting cap are also worn.

DRESS FOR ALL SORTS OF SPORTS

Bowls is a favorite game in the country, and during the Lenten season, where there are a number of clubs formed for its enjoyment.

Although the sessions are in the evening, the men dress at clubs in *mufti* or *negligé*, the golf or cycling suits being the favorites. When you are asked to play bowls at a private house, and when there is a dance to follow, or when you are asked to a "bowling party," it is perhaps better form to wear your dinner jacket or Tuxedo, as there will be supper and dancing afterward. The presence of ladies will not deter you from wearing on an occasion like this demitoilet or dinner jacket, as there is a certain informality about all athletic sports. The same may be said of *badminton*, another favorite Lenten game, played somewhat after the manner of tennis. The difference is that instead of racquet and ball, battledore and shuttlecock are used.

For *skating*, even at a rink on artificial ice, golf costume or *mufti* is good form.

Polo has likewise no code of etiquette not connected with the rules of the game. The dress for polo includes buckskin knee breeches, flannel or madras shirt with low turn-down collar, top riding boots, and polo cap.

SAILING INTO THE SUNSET

A yacht in commission is the most expensive and luxurious toy a man can have. No one but a millionaire can afford it. True, as in other possessions, there are degrees, and consequently there are yachts and yachts. Only large schooner or steam yachts, however, are adaptable for entertaining. A man's yacht is indeed his castle, and the host has only to follow the rules which govern social functions to be perfect in this delightful method of entertaining. Yet there are a few little details of which it would be prudent to speak. The proper entertainments for a yacht in harbor are luncheons, dinners, dances, and short cruises. None of these should be elaborate, the yacht itself—a thing of joy and beauty—being alone a great attraction.

Your sailors should meet the people invited at the dock in the cutter, and row them to the place where your yacht rides at anchor. You should be at the gangway ready to receive them. The same order should be observed on their leaving.

During a club cruise there are several formalities to be observed. You are then as if under military or naval orders. The commodore should be treated with the same consideration as an admiral. You should not appear before him except in the uniform of the club, and you should always salute him on passing, and he should have precedence at all entertainments.

Yachting dress for men consists in either blue flannel or serge suit, or weather pilot or pea-jacket of rough cloth or "witney," or blue serge or flannel coat with naval white duck trousers. The cap, blue or white cloth or duck. White flannels are also worn, but they are not so appropriate. In the evening, usual formal landsman's costume.

There are a few rules of practical yachting which are so intimately connected with etiquette that, although it is not exactly in my province, I propose to give a summary of them here.

When on a cruise, all yachts belonging to a club should hoist their colors at eight o'clock A. M. and haul them down at sunset, taking time from the senior officer present in port, if there should be one. Between sunset and colors they should carry a night pennant. Guns should only be fired on setting or hauling down the colors, except by the yacht giving the time, nor between sunset and colors, nor on Sunday, and the rules of many yacht clubs insist on these formalities being observed whether a yacht is on a cruise or not.

The senior officer in port should be in command, and should make colors and sunset and return salutes and visits, etc. His yacht should remain the station vessel until a senior to him in rank arrives, when such senior should assume the duties of the anchorage.

Flag officers should display their pennants while in commission, except when absent for more than forty-eight hours. In this case their private signal should be hoisted. A blue rectangular flag at the starboard spreader should be displayed when the owner is not on board.

All salutes should be returned in kind. Yachts passing at sea should salute each other, juniors saluting first. This is done by dipping the ensign three times or by firing a gun, followed by dipping the ensign. Arriving in harbor after sunset or on Sunday the salute should be made the first thing next morning.

When a squadron or a cruising expedition enters a port or anchorage and finds there a foreign yacht, the senior officer of the squadron or cruise should send its owner a tender of the civilities of the club. All vessels are considered foreign not belonging to the interstate squadron, or to a club not included in the association of yachts to which your vessel and you belong.

Of course I have only skimmed through the sailing and saluting regulations. You are supposed to have a book of your club, which will give them to you, and you are bound to follow the rules laid down therein.

As a rule, the commodore of a yacht club wears on his cap an anchor one inch and a half in diameter, placed horizontally, embroidered in gold, with a silver star of half an inch diameter at each end of and above the anchor. A vice commodore wears only a single star; captains two crossed foul anchors. The dress uniform of most yacht clubs is a plain blue or black dress coat, a white dress waistcoat, each with the club button in gilt; blue or white trousers with cravat black or white. The undress consists of a double-breasted sack coat of blue cloth, serge, or flannel, blue or white waistcoat, each with the black club button; trousers of same material, or of white drill. The commodore has five black silk stripes on his cuff, the vice commodore four, the rear commodore three, the captain and other officers two, and the members one.

Your crew should wear shirts of blue flannel or white linen with wide blue cuffs and collars, stitched with blue or white thread. Handkerchiefs should be of black silk, caps of blue cloth without visor; straw hats with black ribbon can be used for summer. The name of the yacht must be worked on the breast of the shirt, or printed upon the band of the cap or the ribbon of the hat. The trousers should be of blue flannel or white linen duck. No braces are worn.

HOLE IN ONE

The etiquette of *golf* is incorporated, more or less, with the technicalities of the rules governing the game. I do not intend to go into these, but to give a few hints to the novice, to prevent him, if possible, committing solecisms.

Golf has a vocabulary of its own. The "grounds" on which the game is played is a stretch of rather rough country, abounding in hills, hillocks, and sandy downs, and is known by no other name but the "links."

The game is usually played by two persons, but it can be by more. It consists in driving a ball, small and black, or painted red for the winter snows, along a route laid out by a series of holes to a goal, with a selection of clubs with metal ends. A small boy carries these clubs around for the players. He is called the "caddie."

The clubs have various names and various uses. They are for propelling or driving the ball, according to the rules of the game. They are the driver, long spoon, short spoon, putter, iron putter, cleek, iron, niblick, brassey, lofting iron, and mashie.

A "tee" is a small mound of sand or earth upon which the ball rests. As before explained, the ball is propelled or driven from the tee into one of the holes. The term "putting" is applied to the locality in which this operation of driving the ball into the hole takes place.

The etiquette of the spectator is embraced in the common-sense essential of being an onlooker and nothing more. Silence is golden. Advice and comment, should you profess to know anything about the game, are brazen. Be considerate; do not interfere with the comfort of the players. As at billiards, the stroke should be made in utter silence. The golf "links" is not a place for criticism, and if you are allowed to follow the players around, you must control your feelings alike when enthusiastic or when contemptuous. Besides being a breach of good manners, remember that golf is more or less an outdoor game of whist.

Golf is the easiest game at which to cheat, but as it is a sport in the *repertoire* of a gentleman, it would seem almost an insult to hint at such a contingency. However, apart from the moral effect of cheating at any game, if a man is dead to all sense of honor, he should be alive to the fear of being found out. Such discovery means social ostracism.

The proper golf costume is based on common sense. The man who rigs himself up for this or any other sport in what he considers the most approved style is either a very bad player or a novice. The championships have been won by men wearing their ordinary street costumes or business lounge suits. The English and Scotch golf dress, however, is sack coat, knickers without leather extensions, and a plain tweed shooting cap. The shirt is white madras, soft, unstarched bosom, with a golf stock or Ascot. Golf shoes or boots are of heavy russet or black leather. The hose has a long ribbed top, which is turned over, forming a sort of heavy band on the calf of the leg. It is made of heavy worsted, plain or ribbed. This costume will do for winter in the English climate, when you can not employ too heavy tweeds in the north and west. The American costume, however, is made of lighter tweeds for the spring and autumn, and of brown linen or holland for the summer. As yet, except in one or two localities, golf is not generally played in winter, except by enthusiasts.

At a match, golfers wear their club uniform coats, which are made of hunting pink with brass buttons. The club dress uniform is full and proper dress for all golf functions, such as dinners and dances and receptions. For golf club evening functions, black silk or lisle thread stockings and pumps and black knickers would be appropriate dress. This will be regulated by the rules of the club.

BOATING AND BATHING, TENNIS AND RACING

But a word, and this on costume. The proper dress in England, where *boating* is a social amusement, is the blazer madras shirt with white linen all-around collars and madras cuffs, same material as shirt, white duck trousers, and straw hat with colored ribbons.

For *bathing*, the present ocean costume is all plain, one dark-color two-piece suit, short trousers coming to the knees, and jersey with very short sleeves.

For *tennis*, which I have omitted in the category of sports, as there is no peculiar etiquette attached, you should wear white duck trousers, a white madras shirt, white flannel coat, plain or finely striped, and straw hat or flannel cap to match coat. The straw hat was in vogue last summer.

In England many men wear gray vicuña frock coats to the races. About this costume, however, in America, where races are but seldom social functions, you must be guided by the season, circumstances, and place. Of course, a top hat must be worn with any species of frock coat, but the gray top hat has gone out of fashion.

Gymkhana races are burlesque affairs imported from India. The participants are dressed in grotesque fancy costumes, and are obliged to race holding umbrellas, toy balloons, or some other absurdity. They are in great favor at summer watering places.

BILLIARDS

The etiquette of this popular pastime is possibly embraced in the general maxim of "the extending of the utmost consideration for others."

Billiards constitutes quite an important factor in club life, and should have been included in the chapter on that subject but for the fact that so many private houses have billiard rooms, and the game is better classified with the different sports of a bachelor.

At the club it is allowable to play the game *sans* one's coat, or in shirt sleeves. The billiard room is a place where one can be unconventional. Order, however, in a match game especially, should be strictly maintained. The severe English rule at clubs, under such circumstances, requires the man who has played his stroke "to retire to a reasonable distance, and keep out of the line of sight" (*vide* the Badminton treatise on the game). Orders for drinks to the waiter, loud talking, criticism of the play, lighting pipes and cigars—the latter being only generally allowed in New York club billiard rooms—are all offenses against etiquette.

In private houses it is certainly a breach of good manners to bolt into a billiard room while a game is in progress, except between the strokes, and this period can be easily ascertained by listening at the door. The ideal game is conducted with strict observance of the etiquette of the room. It is, according to the same Badminton authority, a game during the progress of which neither player smokes nor interrupts the other, and spectators are generally courteous, silent, and impartial. In a private house where ladies are apt to be present and to be players, shirt sleeves are certainly not tolerated. The dinner coat is useful on these occasions. Smoking is permissible if the hostess consents.

A MODEL OF SPORTSMANSHIP

The etiquette of *cards* calls for but a word. Whist means silence. No gentleman quarrels with a billiard marker or a golf caddie; still less should he dispute a point at cards. Better lose, especially when women are present, than enter a controversy.

Chapter XVII

A BACHELOR'S TRAVELS AT HOME AND ABROAD

SEEMING AT EASE

To seem entirely at one's ease is the best maxim I can give for traveling. You can not actually pretend to experience that which may be totally lacking, but by making yourself comfortable you will increase the pleasure of others. There is, in these days of luxurious traveling, but little occasion to be flurried, and no excuse whatever for not being as well dressed as you are calm and self-possessed. Dress means a great deal, and if you have not a servant with you it will simply require a little care at the commencement to insure your entire freedom from all annoyance.

CLOTHES, TOILETRIES AND A LITTLE BRANDY

As I have already observed in a previous chapter, in a long journey it would be better to take more than one trunk, but even if you have but the one you should carry also a bag with your toilet articles. A dressing bag is most requisite, and if you can not afford this you could have an ordinary bag, or even a "dress suit" case, fitted up with the necessary appliances of the toilet. These, it is almost absurd to state, consist of your razors, tooth and nail brushes, combs and hairbrushes, individual soap, and a few small vials of very useful physic, such as Jamaica ginger, Pond's extract, liver pills, cologne, and, if you do not carry it in your pocket, a brandy flask. There are times when this is absolutely necessary. In my dressing bag, if possible, I would take my pyjamas, so as to be perfectly equipped for the night, in case, at the end of my journey, I could not get at my trunk. Overcoats, waterproof coat, umbrellas, walking sticks, etc., should be carried in a shawl strap, where you could also have a novel or so, or a budget of interesting newspapers or magazines. For short railway or steamer journeys, the best dress is the ordinary lounge or morning sack suit, with a soft felt or Hombourg hat. Gloves are necessary. Tan or gray suede is the most correct. In winter an ulster should be worn. Select for sea or for ocean voyages the warmest lounge suit you have, or, if you feel more disposed, a warm tweed knickerbocker suit, such as you wear for golf. I think it is a good principle to put on your old clothes at sea. Only very vulgar people dress for this occasion. For late dinner on the ship I would have a black cutaway coat and a light tie. I believe men must change their clothes before dinner at all places and under all circumstances. Russet shoes are worn.

A TIP FROM THE AUTHOR

Do not hurry. Have your tickets purchased in time, and arrive at a train so that you will have fully five minutes in which to check your luggage.
On an ocean voyage, if the ship is going to leave at an early hour in the morning, go on board the night before.

PREPARING FOR YOUR SEA VOYAGE

Farewell suppers are like greetings in tugboats and other vulgar celebrations, the meed of the second-class politician. Arrange with your banker for letters of credit, and take with you just sufficient small change to carry you comfortably and pay your little expenses, with one note of a larger denomination in case of accident. Do not get your money changed on the ship. It is effected at a very high rate of discount. Thus on English ships—the Cunard, White Star, Anchor, and Allan lines—English currency is used. The Hamburg and the North German Lloyd employ German, and the Transatlantique, French. Your steamer trunk and your bag and shawl strap should be placed in the cabin with you. Steamer chairs, in these days, can be hired. Do not carry one around with you. It is a nuisance. On the ocean steamers the steward will attend to your little wants, and prepare your bath for you in the morning, for which there is a fee. It is customary on leaving a ship to give gratuities to servants. To the cabin steward on English ships, ten shillings, the head steward ten shillings, and your waiter ten shillings.

RULES OF TIPPING

Servants abroad are feed on a regular tariff, which you will find in the guidebooks. In this country the drawing-car fiend expects twenty-five cents for a day's journey; fifty cents to a dollar for longer and more extended service. At hotels the waiters are tipped when you leave, and a small gratuity given to chambermaids.

MEETING AND ACCOMPANYING LADIES ON YOUR TRAVELS

Courtesy, especially to women, is the one thing expected from every gentleman who travels, and if you can assist any one in distress by advice or by help of any kind do so, particularly if it is an unprotected woman. But be very guarded in making new acquaintances. Such as are picked up on the steamer, for instance, can be dropped as soon as you land. Beware of the cardroom and the poker sharps who travel on the great liners. Make it a rule, if you will play for money, never to do so with strangers.

When traveling with a lady, always carry her bag and assist her in and out of the trains. Your behavior is on its mettle under these circumstances, and traveling is very apt to be like a mustard plaster, bringing out both the good and evil attributes of a man.

THE ENGLISH AS FOREIGNERS

The subject of foreign travel also needs a few words as well a bit of general advice. English customs and our own are so much alike that it would be strange, indeed, if an American could not get along in the land where his own tongue is spoken. One of the first difficulties which once beset traveling Americans in London was the regulation in theaters that the audience, or that part of it occupying the best stalls, should be in evening dress. As evening dress is now also the rule in New York, this quandary is a thing of the past. Programmes at many of the English theaters are now free, where some years ago it was customary to sell bills of the play for sixpence.

The feeing of servants at hotels, however, continues, and we yet have the charge on hotel bills for service. You are expected to give something to the hall porter, to your waiter, to the boots, and to the chambermaid. The amount of these fees differs according to the length of your stay. I should say a half crown to the porter and less sums to the others.

In London a shilling a mile is the accepted price for cabs within a certain metropolitan radius called the "circle." "Thrupence" or sixpence extra is the tip "to drink your health."

Afternoon dress is the correct attire for the park after midday, and cabs and hansoms are not seen on the Row during riding and driving hours.

TIPPING AND GETTING BY ABROAD

In Paris you may wear a blue blouse and make the turn of the Bois in a *fiacre*. The tariff there is two francs an hour, or two francs fifty per course, from one place to another. The *pourboire* is fifty centimes.

In France the *pourboire* is a veritable tax, as it is in Italy and in the Latin countries. In Germany the mark is equal to about twenty-five cents of our money, and it will go a long way. Ten marks will fee a houseful of servants.

At the station in Paris fifty centimes is given to the porter. The "commissionaire" at the hotel expects fifty centimes. Waiters' *pourboires* are eighty-five centimes at breakfast, and at dinner a franc. In a *café* they are twenty-five centimes.

The woman at the theater who puts a footstool under your feet expects one franc, and at many of the playhouses she must be feed for a reserved seat.

In Paris the orchestra stalls are occupied only by men. At the opera during the season evening dress in the boxes and stalls is, of course, *de rigueur*. At the Comédie Française on Tuesdays and at the Odéon on Thursdays you must be in evening dress in order to gain admittance.

Chairs are sold in Paris at the Catholic churches, and in both the London and Paris parks seats can be hired for a few pennies or sous.

In Paris omnibuses only the seating capacity is allowed. When the omnibus is full, a sign, "*Complet*," is fastened on the outside.

At the gates of each small town in France the *octroi*, or impost, levies on articles of food brought in, and the customhouse in England seizes all American reprints of English books. There, as well as in France, spirits and tobacco are dutiable.

It is only civil to bow when passing the Prince of Wales or members of the royal family. In Paris every hat is removed when a hearse passes, as also in Italy. In Germany the hat is removed when the emperor passes.

Passports are necessary for Russian and Eastern travel.

All large functions on the Continent, no matter what time of the day they occur, demand evening dress. In Paris the bridegroom at a wedding in the afternoon wears evening dress, as well as the chief male mourner at a funeral, but the others present do not. This does not apply to groomsmen and honorary pallbearers, who are in evening dress. In Germany, Austria, and Italy, wherever royalty appears, evening dress is necessary. At the audiences granted by the Pope all men must be in evening dress, and the women in dark gowns and veils.

A ROYAL OCCASION

The Queen of England, the Princess of Wales, and all other female members of the royal family are addressed as "Ma'am"; the Prince of Wales and the male members as "Sir," and never, except by tradesmen, as "Your Royal Highness."

The English dukes are addressed simply as "Duke" and not as "Your Grace"; a marquis is "Lord" and a marchioness "Lady." Younger sons of dukes should be spoken of as lord. A French duke and duchess are addressed as "Monsieur" and "Madame." In Germany one drops the Von when addressing a nobleman who has that title, but when you write to him you must give him his full credentials.

A foreign bishop is always addressed as "My Lord" and a cardinal as "Your Eminence."

The etiquette at a house where the Prince of Wales or a member of the royal family in England visits is rigorous, and on the Continent, when royalty is present, it is even more severe. The prince is never addressed unless he speaks to you. He alone has the privilege of changing the subject of conversation, and all plans for the day's recreation are submitted to him.

Chapter XVIII

THE ENGAGED BACHELOR

MAKING A PROPOSAL

A man should never ask a woman to marry him unless he has the wherewithal to support her in the manner in which she has been accustomed to live. An inquiry into the state of the proposed son-in-law's finances is perfectly proper and should not be taken amiss.

A man is not at liberty to announce his engagement until his *fiancée* gives him permission to do so. It is her family who have the right to know first of the existence of an engagement. Very few engagements are entered into so hurriedly as not to be anticipated in a way by the members of the young woman's household. However, the first step to be taken is the announcement by the *fiancée* to her mother, her father, or her proper guardian of the existing circumstances. Sometimes this is done in a most informal way by both parties. The day after the engagement has thus been announced it is good form for the man to have a private talk with the young woman's parents or guardian.

MAKING IT PUBLIC

Engagements are announced to other members of the family than those of the household by informal notes when it is decided it should be made public. Relatives and intimate friends should be apprised of it before one's general acquaintances. In these days of "society news" the general announcement is frequently made through the medium of the newspapers. It can also be made verbally.

During the engagement it is expected that a man's relatives and friends should pay the prospective bride as much attention as possible. They should call on her and felicitate her as soon as they have been informed of the affair. A pretty compliment for a male member of the man's family or one of his intimates is to send flowers to the new *fiancée*. Engagements should never be announced unless the wedding day is fixed approximately. Avoid long engagements.

AN APPROPRIATE ENGAGEMENT RING

The engagement ring is a solitaire diamond, but one with two smaller diamonds is appropriate. This will depend upon the income of the swain. Rings with colored stones, however, are not in vogue for engagements.

KEEPING UP APPEARANCES

During the engagement the betrothed couple should be seen as much as possible in each other's society. Neither should appear at large entertainments to which the other has not been asked. Little attentions are expected. A man should send from time to time, according to the state of his finances, flowers, sweets, or other tokens. A sensible girl will not approve of costly gifts if you can not afford them. A very acceptable token would be a bunch of violets or American beauty roses sent from a fashionable florist.

Chapter XIX

THE BACHELOR'S WEDDING

NO LONGER A BACHELOR

When a bachelor marries the arrangement of the details of the ceremony and reception are left to the bride's family, and there is really very little about which to instruct him. Many men wish to know how these matters should be conducted, and a short review is here given under the penalty of its being not within the scope of *The Complete Bachelor*.

THE RUDIMENTS

Weddings in society are celebrated either at church or at the home of the bride. The church wedding is the most popular, and in large cities the most fashionable, as it admits of the presence of a large number of people and lends much solemnity to the occasion.

The fashionable hour for a wedding is from high noon—midday—until five o'clock. Evening weddings have within the past five years not been as much in vogue as formerly.

THE INVITATIONS

The invitations are issued within a fortnight of the ceremony. The formula is an announcement engraved on a sheet of heavy cream paper folded in two. It is issued in the name of the bride's parents or guardian, and it requests the pleasure of the guest's presence at the marriage of their daughter or ward at such a church or such a number, at such an hour of the day, month, and year. A separate card, inclosed, with the announcement and invitation to the church, states the hours of the reception. The invitations are very simple, engraved in plain English script, and the paper and cards are of a standard quality known to stationers for this purpose. The inner one is addressed only with the name of the person invited, the outer one has this and the street, the street number, and full directions for mailing. Gilt-edged or fancy stationery is vulgar.

I herewith append some examples. The English invariably insist on the R. S. V. P., or "answer if you please," on even church invitations. The reason for this is that in England those asked to the church are always expected also at the reception. Only the bridal party sit down to an elaborate breakfast, the other guests being given the very lightest of refreshments.

American form:

> *Mr. and Mrs.* ——
> *request your presence*
> *at the marriage of their daughter*
> *Katherine*
>
> *to*
>
> *Mr.* ——,
> *Thursday, February the twenty-eighth,*
> *at twelve o'clock.*
> *Grace Church,*
> *Broadway and Tenth Street.*

Also:

Mr. and Mrs. ——
request the honor of your presence
at the marriage of their daughter
Annie
to
Mr. ——
on (etc.).

Mr. and Mrs. ——
request your presence
at the marriage of their daughter
Myra Raymond
to
Mr. ——,
Thursday, February the twenty-eighth,
at twelve o'clock.
Grace Church,
Broadway and Tenth Street.

Mr. and Mrs. ——
request the honor of your presence
at the marriage of their daughter
Annie
to
Mr. ——
on Tuesday morning, November twenty-seventh,
at half past eleven o'clock.
St. Leo's Church,
East Twenty-eighth Street.

———

Please present this card at
St. Leo's Church,
November twenty-seventh.

English form:

Mr. and Mrs. ———
request the pleasure of
Lord and Lady ———'s
company at
St. Peter's, Eaton Square,
on Saturday, November 4th, at two o'clock,
on the occasion of the marriage of their daughter
Margaret and ——— ———,
and afterward at 1 Grosvenor Square.
R. S. V. P.

———

Admit bearer
to
St. Peter's Church, Eaton Square,
on November 4th, 1895, at two o'clock.

If the bride whom a bachelor is marrying is a widow and lives in her own house, the invitations to the church and the reception, or to either or both, would read simply, "The pleasure of your company is requested at the wedding," etc., with a separate card bearing the word reception and stating the hour and address.

Should there be no guests at the wedding, and should it be conducted very quietly or privately, it is necessary that announcement cards be sent out after the event has taken place. These are issued in the name of the bride's parent, parents, or guardian, who simply announce "the marriage of their daughter [or ward] Elizabeth to Mr. Henry Smith Walcott, Thursday, June the twentieth, eighteen hundred and ninety-six." In the left-hand corner is placed the address of those sending out the cards. A card is also inclosed with the names of the newly married couple, their address, and their reception day. Should there be neither parents nor guardians, the parties to the contract can announce it themselves with one card thus: "Mr. William Benham Thorne and Miss Eleanore Taylor, married on Thursday, November the seventh, eighteen hundred and ——, New York." Another card can also be inclosed, on which is the new address of the married couple, as well as their day at home. If it is a church wedding, and there are neither guardians nor parents, you can use the form, "You are invited to be present at the wedding of ——," etc.

A too rigid economy should not be observed in the sending of wedding invitations, and the prospective bridegroom should see that this is carried out. In case there are several members of a family, it is good form to inclose an invitation to each; thus, Mr. and Mrs. Algernon Smith, the Misses Smith, and Messrs. Smith making three smaller envelopes inclosed in the larger one addressed to Mr. and Mrs. Algernon Smith.

As I have advised in the chapter on Cards, your pasteboard should be left at the house of those in whose name the invitations are issued, even if you are asked only to the church. If to the reception, you owe two visits of "digestion"—one to the bride's parents and one to the happy pair.

FINANCES

All the expenses pertaining to a wedding are borne by the bride's parents. The bridegroom, however, pays the clergyman's fee and provides his own carriage, cab, or hansom from his rooms to the church. This vehicle is also sent to the house of the best man.

All expenses after the marriage are, of course, defrayed by the bridegroom. It has been strict etiquette for the bride and bridegroom not to use the family carriage, which usually takes them from the church, to fetch them to the railroad station, but one provided by the bridegroom. It is frequently a matter of courtesy for the bride's parents to offer this for the occasion.

THE BRIDEGROOM'S DUTIES

The bridegroom should, as soon as the wedding day is appointed, choose his best man and his ushers. The vogue is to ask his nearest unmarried male relative or his most intimate bachelor friend to serve in the capacity of best man. More recently a number of very fashionable New Yorkers have had married men take that position, and thus the innovation has sanction through the action of the "smart set." A married best man is said to be an English fad, but I find that it could be more correctly termed an Anglo-Indian mode, as this new idea is much more popular in Calcutta and Bombay than in London.

In the selection of ushers, a man asks usually some few of his intimates or club friends, and through courtesy to his prospective bride a male member of her family, frequently her brother. Six ushers are the usual number, although four are quite sufficient. Some few men have been known to dispense with the services of the best man and have only ushers, but this is not exactly correct at a fashionable church wedding. The ushers can be very easily omitted if the ceremony is to take place at the house.

The bridegroom presents his best man and his ushers with their ties, their gloves, and tie pin, which is a souvenir of the occasion, as well as their *boutonnières*, or "buttonholes," to accept the last English expression, to be worn at the ceremony.

The tie, gloves, and tie pin are given to the best man and the ushers at the farewell bachelor dinner; the *boutonnières* are ordered at the florist's and sent to them on the morning of the wedding. Lilies of the valley are the favorite wedding flowers, but the floral arrangements are regulated by the bride's family, who possibly have a certain color or flower scheme for the church decorations, and the "buttonholes" must be in keeping.

The bridegroom generally provides hansoms or *coupés* to drive his ushers to the church from their respective residences. As the bride's family provides the carriages for the *cortège*, these other vehicles may be dismissed at the church.

The bridegroom himself drives to the church in a hansom with his best man.

If it is a house wedding these carriages need not be provided. In this country the *bridegroom* does not give the bridesmaids any token or present. In England he presents them with brooches or bracelets. In New York the bride presents her maid of honor and bridesmaids with souvenirs in the shape of lace pins, brooches, or bracelets.

The bridegroom always gives to his bride a handsome wedding present, which is to be worn or carried on the happy day. It may be a diamond tiara, it may be a diamond star, it may be jewels of any kind which he can ascertain would be acceptable to her, or it may be a prayer book. *The bridegroom* does not provide any part of the bride's costume.

If the bride should carry flowers instead of a prayer book, this special bouquet is the gift of the bridegroom, but the flowers for the bridesmaids are provided by the bride.

The expenses of the wedding notices in the newspapers and the fee to the clergyman are paid by the bridegroom through the agency of the best man.

The wedding ring is of bright burnished gold, perfectly plain. The date of the wedding and the initials of the happy pair should be engraved on the inside. The ring is confided to the best man, who produces it at the proper time during the ceremony.

It is customary for a prospective bridegroom to purchase or, rather, to have a wedding outfit made. Very elaborate affairs of this kind are not in good taste, and anything which suggests the occasion is certainly vulgar. Beyond the clothes for the ceremony, there should be a general overhauling of the wardrobe and shirts, undervests, underclothes, handkerchiefs, and such articles must, if any of them are needed or have fallen into decay, be supplied or renewed. All this is a matter of taste.

THE FAREWELL DINNER

The bachelor farewell dinner is now a recognized institution. Perhaps next to the ceremony itself, it is regarded as the most important social function of the wedding week.

If you are a member of a club, your farewell dinner should be given there in one of the private dining rooms. Otherwise it is perfectly correct to have it at a well-known restaurant or hotel, in, of course, a private dining room. You may have it at your own house, and, should your parents be living and you reside with them, it can be given at home. The club, however, is really first choice. Sometimes the strictly bachelor dinner is dispensed with, and in its stead a dinner is given to the entire bridal party by the family of the bride. This does away with the presumed selfishness of the "stag" dinner, and the possible excuse for some one or more of the guests to become exhilarated—a *finale*, I am grieved to say, that has happened on more than one occasion.

At the stag dinner you should have your best man, your ushers, and several of your friends. You can invite a married man or so, especially if he is a very jolly fellow, and it is expected that some one or more of your bride's relatives will be included. Twelve is a good number, but, of course, never thirteen, because women are generally superstitious, and should this become known to your future one it might cause her great mental anxiety.

FAVORS AND TABLE LAYOUT

The gloves, ties, and tie or scarf pins to be given to the best man and ushers are placed in white boxes tied with white satin ribbon and put in the outer room to be handed to each man as he bids adieu. Perhaps it might be more prudent to place them at the covers, but it would hardly be good form, as there would be in that case several of the guests without favors. And, besides, a dinner with favors is not permissible in these days.

Boutonnières of lilies of the valley should be also placed at each cover. The *menu* cards should be simple but tasteful. Elaborate *menus* are not now in the best form. In fact, with a bachelor dinner, as with all functions of this kind, elegant simplicity should be the predominating characteristic; cut glass and silver are all that is required. In the center of the table a basket, or, better, a silver *jardinière* of roses, is the only floral decoration. During the course of the dinner these flowers are removed and are sent to the bride-elect. It is sometimes the custom—and a very pretty one—for each guest to note a sentiment on a *menu* card or simply his own name, and have that sent also with the flowers.

CHOOSING THE MENU

The dinner itself can, but need not be very elaborate. I do not like a dinner of many courses. It is usual to serve sherry and whisky and caviare sandwiches in the anteroom before dinner, and also to have cigars and cigarettes galore there as well as at table, although it is not permissible to smoke before the cheese is served. I would recommend raw oysters, a clear soup, a bit of fish with sliced cucumber—an attractive *entrée*; a *fillet* with vegetables, canvas-back duck, cheese and salad, coffee, and fruit.

THE CEREMONY

On the morning of the wedding the bridegroom is called for in the hansom or cab which has been ordered for himself and the best man. The best man calls for him and takes him to the church. They should time their movements so as to arrive at least five minutes before the hour appointed for the ceremony. The same precaution should be observed if it is a house wedding.

At day weddings afternoon dress is *de rigueur* for bridegroom, best man, ushers, and all male guests. The bridegroom, best man, and ushers should be dressed alike in frock coats and waistcoats to match, trousers of dark gray striped, patent-leather shoes, gray suede gloves, white or pearl-colored scarfs, and top hats.

The English have allowed some latitude, and wear gray frock coats and even colored shirts, but this fashion is not generally in vogue in America. Evening weddings require formal evening dress. A wedding at dusk in winter, where the bride wears traveling costume, calls for afternoon dress on the part of the bridegroom.

The bridegroom and best man alight at the vestry. They remain in the back of the chancel until the first notes of the wedding march notify them of the presence of the bride. The best man must see before the ceremony that the bridegroom's top hat, as well as his own, is sent to the entrance of the church to be handed to the respective owners on their exit.

When the bride, on the arm of her father or guardian, approaches the altar, the bridegroom and best man walk out from the vestry, either together or the best man in advance. In the latter case the best man steps back at the chancel rail, and allows the bridegroom to pass before him. The bridegroom stands on the right-hand side of the altar or reading desk and the best man on his right. The bride is on the bridegroom's left, and her father or guardian a little behind her on her left.

To avoid confusion, the ceremony is generally rehearsed an evening or two before. Much depends on the liturgy of the communion to which the couple belong. The best man has charge of the ring, and must produce it and hand it to the clergyman at the time it is demanded.

At the conclusion of the ceremony the best man precedes the bride and bridegroom in the procession, escorting the maid of honor, unless the *cortège* has been differently arranged. In that case, he makes his way either through the vestry or down one of the aisles to the church door, where he superintends the filing away of the bridal carriages and party. At the reception he goes in to breakfast with the maid of honor, or with a near relative of the bride's family. He may use the bridegroom's hansom from the church to the house, or he may go with one of the family. There is no rule for this. The bride and bridegroom use the bride's carriage.

The best man is intrusted also with the paying of the clergyman. The bridegroom will give him a check for this purpose. As already stated, he also inserts the marriage notices in the newspapers, the funds for which are also provided by the bridegroom. He pays his own personal expenses.

The ushers meet in the church about an hour before the ceremony. The bridegroom generally puts carriages at their disposal, but that is not in the least obligatory. They can take hansoms or cabs, or for that matter go to the rendezvous in the car or stage. The ushers stand at the foot of the nave or aisle and busy themselves escorting guests to seats. An usher offers his right arm to the lady he escorts up the aisle. Even if a lady should be accompanied by her husband or escort, the usher should offer her his arm, and the other man walks up behind them. If an usher should not have had the formality of an introduction to the lady he is showing to a seat, a bow and a smile when leaving her is all that is necessary. An usher, being a friend of the family, knows those who ought to go beyond the ribbon and those who are not relatives or family connections. The bride's brothers, if they are ushers, take care of the members of their family, and the intimate friends of the bridegroom or his relations. The relatives of the bride are placed in the front pews beyond the ribbon on the right-hand side of the altar, and the bridegroom's on the left-hand side. At the arrival of the bridal party the

ushers get together and form in the back of the church for
the procession up the aisle or nave. Their meeting thus
is the cue for the sexton, who signals the organist, and
the march is started. The ushers advance up the aisle, two
by two, until they reach the chancel, where they divide
on the right and on the left, allowing the bridesmaids to
pass before them, standing in a semicircle around the altar
rails. If it is a Roman Catholic wedding they genuflect
as they reach the chancel. They file down the aisle in
the same order, heading the bridal procession. At the
carriage way they assist the bridesmaids in their carriages,
and by previous arrangement they are allotted to certain
carriages escorting the bridesmaids.

At the reception the bride and bridegroom take their
places under a wedding bell of flowers or in the front
drawing room between the two front windows, or, again,
in the back drawing room. The house is decorated with
palms, potted plants, flowers, and other foliage. Pink and
white orchids, ferns, and chrysanthemums make very
effective decorations. The mother of the bride, or nearest
female relative, stands at the door of the drawing room
and greets the guests. The ushers and bridesmaids are
scattered about the room.

YOUR ROLE AS GUEST

If there is only a reception, then the guests, after
exchanging greetings with the lady of the house, pass on
and shake hands with and congratulate the bridegroom
and wish the bride joy. Unless you are an intimate friend,

do not attempt any set speech. The bride will say, if she has not seen you for a short time before the wedding, "I must thank you, Mr. Smith, for your beautiful present," or something of that kind. If you do not know the bridegroom she will present you to him. If you are a friend of the bridegroom he will present you to the bride, and should say, if such is the case, "Evangeline," or "May," or "Margaret," or otherwise; or "My dear, let me present to you Mr. Algernon Smith, who, you remember, is one of my best friends." And if Mrs. —— has any tact, she will at once reply, "I am so pleased to meet any of my husband's old friends, and I must thank you, Mr. Smith, for the beautiful *bonbon* dishes. They were just what I wanted," or words to that effect. Then pass on. Refreshments are served at a wedding reception from a buffet in the dining room. If you enter with a lady, ask her what she would like, and get it for her. Then take your own choice of refreshment, and stand or sit by her as the accommodations of the room will permit. A half hour at a wedding reception is sufficient. It is not good form to bid good-by to the bride and bridegroom, but only to the lady of the house. If there is no chaperon— for instance, if the bride be a widow or divorcee and is in her own home—then you must bid her good-by, but in such cases large receptions are not given.

THE MORNING AFTER THE CEREMONY

There is always a breakfast or luncheon set for the bridal party, at which the bride, escorted by the bridegroom, leads the way. The bride's father, escorting the bridegroom's mother, the ushers and bridesmaids and relatives follow. In this country we have  no special law of precedence, and these bridal luncheons are more or less informal. There are no toasts.

After breakfast the valet, should there be one, must be ready with the bridegroom's valise, when his master retires to put on a tweed suit for traveling; otherwise it can be laid out by one of the servants. With the coachman on the box and amid the usual shower of rice and slippers, as also the fusillade of a battery of eyes from neighbors' windows, and perhaps a crowd of street urchins and admiring servants, the happy couple start out on their wedding journey. I think it is better taste to wait until dark, almost, so as to avoid all this unseemly publicity, and I am averse to having the coachman and horses decked with white ribbons; but, of course, one does not marry every day in the year, and these little eccentricities are pardonable on such—shall I say?—an "auspicious" occasion.

SMALLER SCALE WEDDINGS

At a home wedding, as has been said above, ushers are not necessary. The same ceremonial is observed as at church, but due allowance must be made for crowded quarters. Usually very few are asked to the ceremony, but many to the reception afterward. As soon as the ceremony is over congratulations are in order, the newly married couple standing under the bell of flowers where they were married, and receiving the good wishes of their friends.

MARRYING ABOARD

If a man marries abroad there are many annoying bits of red tape to be considered. In London you are obliged to have a legal residence in the parish where the ceremony is to be performed. In Paris a civil marriage before the mayor of the district is necessary. Certificates of baptism must be filed with him, and you must give proof of the legal consent of both your parents as well as those of the bride. The religious ceremony takes place twenty-four hours after the civil. It is strict etiquette that the contracting parties do not see each other during this interim.

The order of the wedding procession in France and on the Continent differs vastly from that in England and America. There are neither ushers nor a best man. If there are bridesmaids the groomsmen accompany them. The bride enters on the arm of her father preceded by the attendants, and the bridegroom follows, escorting his future mother-in-law. A long procession of relatives brings up the rear. The men, no matter at what time of the day the ceremony might take place—and evening weddings are unknown—are in formal evening dress.

Under the French law also no widow or divorcee can remarry until ten months have elapsed since the dissolution of the previous contract. This should not be forgotten by bachelors contemplating matrimony with either one of these classes of eligibles. In Germany there are further complications, and I would advise all contemplating matrimony there to consult the consul or minister at the legation.

Chapter XX

FUNERALS

PAYING RESPECTS TO THE
FAMILY OF THE DECEASED

When a death occurs in the house all matters should at once be placed in charge of a relative or a friend of the family. The family itself should be kept away from every one as much as possible, and none of the sad details left to them. They should not be seen until the day of the funeral. Front windows should be shut, blinds and shades pulled down, and the outer or storm door of the house closed. A servant is stationed in the hall near the door, as on reception days, to receive the cards of persons calling. All acquaintances who have been entertained at the house leave cards in person, others may mail them. Only intimate friends of the family are admitted to the house.

SENDING YOUR CONDOLENCES

Should you send flowers, do not purchase or order any set designs. They are hideous—remind one of the tenement funerals, and are strikingly inappropriate. A bunch of white roses or of violets is a beautiful offering for a young woman, or two palms crossed, with violets or lilies of the valley attached, for a man or an elderly person. These should be accompanied by your card. If you have been an intimate friend, a few words written—a short note of condolence—would not be amiss.

ACKNOWLEDGING CONDOLENCES

To all of these notes, and in acknowledgment of these offerings, one of the family nearest the deceased in relationship should respond by sending their card with the words, "Thank you for your kind sympathy," or something of that sort, written upon it.

THE FUNERAL

As a rule, when the deceased is a young man who belongs to several clubs or who has a numerous acquaintance, it is better to have the funeral from a church. Pallbearers are chosen from among his intimate friends; a relative never acts as pallbearer. It is not customary for any except the nearest relatives to go to the cemetery. Ladies of the family do not accompany the remains to the cemetery, and they frequently do not attend the funeral services at the church if the deceased is a man.

If the funeral services are held at the house the relatives and intimate friends are invited into the back parlor, dining room, or upstairs, and make their appearance only when the services begin. The undertaker attends to seating people, arranging the rooms, etc.

STRICT DRESS CODE

There is only one proper dress for a man to wear at a funeral. It should consist of black frock coat, dark trousers, dark scarf and gloves (gray or dark tan, but not black, unless you are a relative), and top hat. Should you be a relative or a pallbearer, wear a black weed on your hat.

MOURNING PERIODS

As to periods of mourning, there seems to be some little difference of opinion. Ward McAllister treated the subject in quite an exhaustive manner, advocating short mourning terms even for the nearest relatives. For a wife eighteen months is considered the proper thing; for a parent, twelve to eighteen months, sometimes two years; for a brother or a sister, one year; and for a grandparent, six months. A maternal or paternal uncle or aunt is entitled to about two months or less, according to the intimacy which has existed between the families. Seclusion from society is generally consonant with mourning for near relatives. However, people now go to the theater and small dinners and teas after nine months of mourning for the very nearest relatives.

MOURNING ATTIRE

It is not necessary for a man to shroud himself in black. A silk hat with a crape band nearly to the top should be worn by widowers during the first year of their widowerhood; but black shirt studs, black sleeve buttons, handkerchiefs bordered with black, and the other abominations in which the grief-stricken Frenchman arrays himself are not tolerated. In deep mourning one can wear black ties and black gloves, but a white linen tie in summer is permissible. I do not advocate the use of black scarf pins.

A black band on the sleeve of a gray suit is also another affectation which should be avoided. Cards should be left after a funeral.

Chapter XXI

MISCELLANEOUS ADVICE

GENERAL ADVICE FOR UNCLASSIFIED OCCASIONS

If you are chosen godfather, you are expected to send a silver mug to your godchild. Christening parties are held about four in the afternoon. Afternoon dress is required.

Even should your friends be among the most exclusive and fashionable in any place, they are never "swells," nor do they belong to the "Four Hundred."

If you send flowers never have them arranged in set designs. Fair voyagers will thank you much more if you send fruit, sweets, or books, as flowers on shipboard or railroad trains are nuisances. Books, sweets, and flowers are the only gifts which a bachelor can offer or a woman accept from him.

The terms "lady" and "gentleman" are distinctive. Your friends and acquaintances are all supposed to be ladies and gentlemen. To distinguish them as such implies a doubt. Should you call at a house you ask if the "ladies" are in, so as to distinguish them from the other females in the household. You also toast the "ladies." In referring to the gentler sex, it is more complimentary to speak of them as "women." You would say, "She is a clever woman," not a "clever lady." The person who speaks of "a lady or a gentleman friend" has a defined social position.

Avoid slang, especially that of the music halls or the comic newspapers. You can well afford not to be "up to date."

In greeting a person say "Good morning," "Good afternoon," or "Good evening," but refrain from such inane phrases as "Delighted, I'm sure." On introduction or presentation, it is sufficient to say "I am delighted to meet you." Avoid also the "How d'y do?" "How are you?" "Very well, I thank you." All this is idiotic.

Whistle all you like in your bedroom, but not in public.

Gentlefolk have "friends" stopping with them, never "company." Servants have and keep "company." When you refer to wine it means any kind of vintage, and not necessarily champagne. Therefore beware of the "gentleman who opens wine," or the one who gives a "wine party," whatever that may mean. We speak of a dinner, but not of a dinner party. A party to the play, no matter where the location of the places may be, is never a "box party."

Do not be a professed jester nor yet a punster. The clowns of society are not enviable beings.

When speaking of a fashionable woman do not refer to her as a "society woman." That would imply that she belongs to various societies or guilds, which is not probably the impression you desire to convey.

When a person has a predilection for the use of the word "elegant," and especially when it is employed in the sense of beautiful, good, charming, or delightful, you are quite just in your estimation of his or her vulgarity.

Answers to questions should be given in the direct affirmative or the direct negative. "All right" is not, to say the least, civil, and is ill-bred.

Never exhibit your accomplishments, unless "by special request," in the public parlors of hotels, or saloons of ships, or other places of general gathering. The persons who sing and play the piano and make themselves bores are as reprehensible as the window opening and shutting fiends, the fidgety travelers, the loud-voiced and constant complaining, all of whom are most obnoxious.

Under great provocation the expletive "damn" is tolerated by society, but it should be whispered and not pronounced aloud. The man who swears is certainly beyond the pale, and the one who uses silly and senseless exclamations is not far away from him. One of the marks of a gentleman is his complete mastery of himself under the most trying and aggravating circumstances.

These are but few of the many "don'ts" which it seems necessary to repeat in works of this kind. For a more extended catalogue of social and grammatical sins, the reader is referred to that excellent book *The Verbalist*, by Alfred Ayres, and the clever little *brochure* Don't. A careful study of these will assist him much in reviewing elementary questions, the knowledge of which was taken for granted by the author of *The Complete Bachelor*.

If you're interested in finding out more about our books, find us on Facebook at **Summersdale Publishers** and follow us on Twitter at @Summersdale.

www.summersdale.com